GW00392319

JO SIFFERT

BY
JACQUES DESCHENAUX

WILLIAM KIMBER · LONDON

First Published in English in 1972 by
WILLIAM KIMBER AND CO. LIMITED
Godolphin House, 22a Queen Anne's Gate
London, S.W.1

ISBN 7183 0402 0

TYPESET BY
SPECIALISED OFFSET SERVICES LTD., LIVERPOOL,
AND PRINTED IN GREAT BRITAIN BY
W. & J. MACKAY & CO. LTD., CHATHAM

CONTENTS

LIST OF ILLUSTRATIONS

FOREWORD

It is with very mixed emotions that I write this foreword and tribute to the memory of the life of *mon cher ami* Seppi. The reason that I have to write it is because he is no longer with us, and this to me is very sad, as he was one of my greatest and dearest friends. To me Seppi Siffert was like a son, and it has been said that he looked upon me as a spiritual father. If this is so, I only hope that it was the right spirit I was giving him.

My other feeling is that, since this tragedy has happened, I am delighted that somebody has taken it upon himself to write this book whilst his memory and the facts of the career of this great personality are still fresh in our minds.

There is nobody better qualified to do this than Jacques Deschenaux, and he has taken infinite pains to speak personally with all those people connected with Seppi, and to check the facts. Jacques for several years lived very close to Siffert, probably more so than anybody else. He was like a personal assistant to him, and he tried to put some order into what was, let's face it, a somewhat disorderly life.

Seppi hardly ever reserved a room in an hotel; if the airport was sixty miles away come rain, fog or snow, Seppi would leave one hour to get there. I know, as I have experienced a journey in the latter conditions. Invariably if he was leaving London Airport we would have to telephone a special number to tell them he was on his way and that he would arrive fifteen minutes before take-off, so that they could count him in on the computer the necessary forty-five minutes beforehand. That it all happened successfully, and that he did arrive and had a bed to sleep in, was usually due to Jacques. He used to arrive at the circuit carrying Seppi's helmet, his gloves, his visor and everything else and I think Seppi took it for granted that Jacques would see that he had all that was needed. And obviously, Jacques came to know him very well. Deschenaux was learning to be a lawyer, but with all Seppi's requirements, how he found time for his studies beats me; however, obviously Siffert came first.

Seppi Siffert came from quite humble surroundings, but at a very youthful age he learnt to take care of himself and his family. He became one of the greatest racing drivers of our time both in sports cars and single-seaters. He was a very astute and brilliant businessman who was completely trustworthy. His word was his bond and no contracts were necessary with him. Above all he was one of Nature's Gentlemen, both charming and courteous. Everybody adored him, particularly the girls.

Seppi enjoyed life to the full. He was always laughing and joking, and my wife and I would tease him endlessly, which he loved. He was very sporting, but the one time he could get upset was if the car went wrong when he was doing well. Then he would sit in the pit like an angry lion cub, but after half and hour it would all be over and he returned to his normal cheerful self having uttered a few *'Merde, alors!'*

Siffert always wanted to join a works team as he felt he would get a more competitive car this way, and probably he was right. So he finally left me after five years together, at the end of the 1969 season. It was a big blow to me, but we still maintained our great friendship. At the Grands Prix he invariably dined with us rather than with his own team. The very weekend that he was killed he was going to stay at our apartment in London, from where he had previously married

Simone, but at the last moment he decided to stay nearer Brands Hatch.

I very much regret that I missed an irretrievable opportunity at Nurburgring; when we were just sitting down to dinner at the Sporthotel, the night before the race, Seppi said to me: 'Would you like me to take you around the circuit in my Porsche now.' Much as I would have adored it, I told him that we would never get back our hard-earned table if we left at that moment, as many people were queuing for it. So I missed out on what would have been an unforgettable experience.

Seppi lived taking part in the sport he loved most and he died doing it, which is the way he would have wanted it; we his friends and admirers are the losers. He was the hero of all Switzerland and they truly showed their affection for him when 50,000 of them turned up to pay tribute to him at his funeral, the like of which I have never seen since that of Sir Winston Churchill.

I hope all those that read this book will get the enjoyment out of it that Seppi Siffert got out of living his life. I always feel that the words of the poet Laurence Binyon are very apt for Seppi Siffert, and all the other drivers who died like him:

They shall grow not old, as we that are left grow old:
Age shall not weary them, nor the years condemn.
At the going down of the sun and in the morning
We will remember them.

Nunney,
May, 1972.

ACKNOWLEDGEMENTS

I have tried to make this biography as accurate as possible. It does not set out to create, or continue, what has come to be called by some the 'Jo Siffert Legend'. My intention was more simple: I felt that his life story was worth telling and I wanted to write about the real man, a person whom I much admired and of whom I am proud to have been a friend.

This portrait of Jo Siffert cannot be exhaustive, but I hope that I have brought out the essential characteristics of his personality. I could not have written this book at all without the help of a great many people and I would like to thank particularly Adelaide Bondanini-Siffert, Yvette Cudry, Josephine Huber, Rachel Noth, Marguerite Ragonesi-Siffert, Maria Siffert, Simone Siffert, Teresa Siffert and Betty Walker. I am also most grateful to the following for their assistance: Chris Amon, Lucien Balsiger, Georges Blanc, Bernard Blancpain, Paul Blancpain, Jo Bonnier, Robert Boschung, Bernard Cahier, Adrianno Cimarosti, Georges Filipinetti, Jean-Claude Fontana, Carlo Frangi, Peter Gethin, Pierre Gross, Gabriel Guisolan, Fredy Haenni, Graham Hill, Franco Lini, Heini Mader, Max Mosley, Jean-Pierre Oberson, Tim Parnell, Jo Pasquier, Xavier Perrot, Michel Piller, Dr Ferry Porsche, David Raymond, Brian Redman, Ugo Schibler, Alois Siffert, Rico Steinemann, Jackie Stewart, Auguste Stritt, Edgar Strub, John Surtees, Ron Tauranac, Jean-Paul Thiemard, Fernand Thorin, Jean Tinguely, Guy von der Weid, Rob Walker, Peter Warr, Eddy Wyss and Alain Zurcher.

CHAPTER ONE

Three men were travelling in a Renault van. At the wheel was Lucien Balsiger, a car-dealer from Geneva and a part-time Formula Junior driver. It was four o'clock on a morning in January 1961. Balsiger — known as Bisule — was on his way from Geneva to England with a friend, Jean Knecht, to take delivery of two Lotus 18s — one for himself and one for Louis Noverraz. The third man, who sat part of the time in the back of the van, and part sitting on the engine cover between the two seats to keep warm, was a young chap of twenty-four. His name was Jo Siffert. Swiss motor cycle champion in 1959 on a Norton 350, the young Fribourgeois had graduated the following year from two wheels to four — acquiring a Fiat-Stanguellini, front-engined, with which he made his four-wheeled debut and won his first hill climb at Cote d'Urcy in France.

It was cold. It was a long trip and Joseph could not make up his mind whether it was more uncomfortable sitting in the dark in the back of the van or perched on the rounded, throbbing engine cover. He wasn't doing it for fun or for kicks — it was the cheapest way to travel. But he didn't feel sorry for himself; he was pondering and perhaps indulging in a few daydreams. He was not at all well off, far from it, and he was getting caught up in one of the most arduous — and expensive — sports there is: motor racing.

15

At the Lotus works Joseph appeared only mildly interested in the single-seaters which, with the Coopers, were then the best in the field. With a detached air he discussed the qualities and particularly the price with Peter Warr. Having negotiated the best discount possible, he placed a firm order for a Lotus 18. The decision had been taken before he left Switzerland but the price was far above his means. The racing car would cost him 18,400 Swiss francs — every penny he could make working hard right through the winter. By a bit of good luck, and because there was a certain sale for the car if he failed to make it, the instalments quoted were not prohibitive and Joseph did not have to make a huge deposit.

The return journey was less daunting: his mission satisfactorily concluded and with the extra weight of the Noverraz and Balsiger cars, the van bumped less. One Lotus was in the back and the other on a trailer. There were more problems in the offing but for the moment Joseph was not thinking about them; sitting in the dark in the driving seat of Bisule's Lotus 18 he pictured himself in a few months' time in the cockpit of his own car.

Two months later, Saturday the 18th March, Siffert was in an appalling temper. Held up in London, the plane bringing his Lotus would not arrive until the evening, too late to clear Customs. And the next day there was a hill-climb for which he had entered at the Mont-sur-Rolle.

'Here I've been pinching and scraping all winter night and day to pay for this wretched car and I can't start in the first race,' he told Gabriel Guisolan.

His friend had a brainwave. 'Councillor Bourgknecht, Minister of Finance and Excise, comes from Fribourg. What if we telephone him?'

'But I don't know him.'

'Nor do I. But let's try!'

And they did. The worthy official's wife advised Gaby to get on to Doctor Lenz, Director-General of Customs, who no

he first motor cycle race—a hill-climb at
Montheron—in which Jo Siffert came
ourth

ictory with Edgar Strub in the Austrian
rand Prix for motor cycle combinations,
958

toire
.P. d'Autriche Zeltweg. 1958

The Lotus 18 which
Siffert drove to victo[ry]
at Cesenatico in 196[1]

Premiere course sur une Lotus Typ. 18. T. et Premier Victoire
circvit de Cesenatico Italie 1961

The first racing car—
the Fiat-Stanguellin[i]

Victory celebration:
Michel Piller, Jo Siff[ert]
Jean-Pierre Oberson
and a friend

doubt impressed by a reference to the earlier telephone call and thinking that he was perhaps talking to friends of the Councillor, made immediate arrangements for the racing car to be passed through the Customs on arrival in spite of it being very late on a Saturday night. At dinner-time that evening 'Group Siffert' left Granges-Paccot on the outskirts of Fribourg in a Ford station wagon towing a trailer, bound for Dubendorf near Zurich: the aeroplane was due to arrive and the Customs officials had been alerted. Almost as soon as it had touched down the Lotus was unloaded, weighed and whisked through the Customs — the Customs men were all under the happy impression that they were assisting people with friends in high places.

In the small hours of the next day Joseph set out again from Fribourg with his two mechanics, Michel Piller and Jean-Pierre Oberson, for Rolle. By now the practice runs over the course were clearly over; they had all been finished the night before. Joseph talked, pleaded, insisted: finally the organizers allowed him to make three ascents. Obviously he needed more than that to get to know the car and the track from Rolle to Gimel, but he could at least take part. Even if he turned in the best time — although a win without any practice would have been a remarkable achievement — under the rules he could not win officially. He did the first climb in 2 minutes 16.7 seconds; the next one was 2 minutes 08.9 seconds, the best time in his class. The fastest time of the day was put in by Harry Zweifel in 2 minutes 06.1 seconds. He was driving a larger 2-litre Cooper. Joseph's third run was hindered by snow and he only reached Gimel in 2 minutes 19.5 seconds.

Joseph was jubilant. His times were not official but what did that matter? He had proved himself, proved that he had taken the right course. He had trounced the opposition. After five or six days of practice and knowing his car perfectly Lucien Balsiger had been sure of beating Joseph by several

17

lengths: 'In fact he knocked two seconds off me — and that certainly showed the gap between us,' Bisule remembered.

* * * * *

Joseph Siffert was born in Fribourg on the 7th July 1936. Not very prosperous, his family had a small dairy business in the middle of the old town next door to the Cafe Tierlibaum in the Place de Petit St Jean near the River Auge.

Standing on the borders of the Sarine, the frontier between the German and French-speaking Swiss, Fribourg is a bilingual town with a population of 40,000 although the majority speak French. Not everyone in fact knows German and if one wants to be understood French is safer because the secrets of the German patois are not easily taken in.

Fundamentally Catholic, the town is the See of a Bishopric taking in Lausanne and Geneva. The University is well known, as well as the picturesque old town and the frank, decided character of its inhabitants.

Joseph's father Alois Siffert came from Wallenbuch and Maria, his mother, was an Ackermann from Willisau in the Canton of Lucerne, so Joseph Siffert would normally have been brought up in the German language. However, his parents' first care for the little Seppi — the diminutive of the German for Joseph — was not learning to speak but to correct a malformation of the right foot, which was completely turned inwards. At six weeks Joseph underwent his first operation at St Anne's Clinic. Doctor Niquille put the child's leg in plaster; for week after week his mother took him to the doctor's consulting room hoping each time that the plaster could be taken off. Joseph took it all very calmly; he certainly felt the extra weight of his imprisoned leg but he didn't cry about it. At six months he couldn't sit up and later he couldn't stand upright except by hanging on to the bars of his cot. Otherwise he just lay there patiently on his back.

18

After a whole year the doctor started to remove the plaster. Lying on his back on a table Seppi felt the foot slip back. It all had to start again. His case was transferred to Professor Dubois in Berne and he carried out a second operation. Joseph spent five days in the Lindenhof Hospital in Berne and then he spent six weeks with a plaster up to mid-thigh. This time the operation was successful. The foot remained straight. His mother was quite overcome — she hadn't dared to hope that all would be well.

But the rehabilitation of the leg wasn't perfect; for the rest of his life Seppi's right leg was shorter than the other and a little thinner which explained his rather curious gait.

Joseph was three when the Second World War broke out. By good fortune, and thanks also to their neutrality and diligent preparation for war, Switzerland was spared. But the threat remained. Alois Siffert was called up. Maria Siffert, Joseph and his little sister Adelaide, only just born, left Fribourg for the farm at Wallenbuch. The men were all under arms; the women worked in the fields. Money was terribly short. Seppi could feel this and he wanted to help. He decided that he ought to sell the tricycle which he had been given for Christmas in 1940. But who to? — the son of a neighbour who had sometimes borrowed it. A deal was soon put through. The purchaser knew where his parents kept some spare cash and there was certain to be 100 francs available — the agreed price. That night Seppi's conscience was not entirely untroubled; he hesitated to produce the 100-franc note which he kept hidden in his hand and which was burning his fingers. The matter was settled with a spanking for both the contracting parties and an immediate return to the status quo.

The Siffert family moved next to Morat. Although she went without meals more and more, Mamma Siffert saw her children getting hungrier and hungrier. Seppi now had two sisters, Adelaide and Marguerite. There just wasn't enough and their mother sold everything that she could, everything that was not essential. One day she came across a silver-plated bread dish which had been a wedding present. But what was the use of a bread dish if there wasn't any bread? Maria Siffert set off for Fribourg on foot, sold the dish for 7 francs to a cousin, and went back on foot to Morat. Over twenty miles on foot for 7 francs — but worth it if it would feed the children.

Joseph was six when his parents went to live in Fribourg again in the Rue du Temple. He was not enchanted with the Infants' School in spite of the kindness of Sister Cunegonde — his heart was not really in it, though he wasn't quite sure where it actually was. The place where he lived, his family background, the way his mother whom he adored had to work just to keep them going, everything seemed wrong to him. Six years old, he wanted to change things and find a new life. He wanted to lift his parents out of the rut and at the same time to find his own way.

He didn't like the German-speaking Primary School at Bourg much better. Joseph was a well behaved pupil but mediocre. Mademoiselle Josephine Huber, his form mistress, thought he was intelligent but why was he always day-dreaming? What was he after? There seemed to be no answer. He just did not make any progress. She always thought of him as the Snail.

'Snails have time for dreaming', she would say.

Arithmetic was particularly disagreeable to Seppi and he would often have to stay in class after four o'clock. When his mother said that she was amazed at the way he would not get involved in school, he would simply reply with a phrase he had perhaps picked up from his form-mistress:

'Churchill didn't do very well at school!'

In fact school didn't interest him except for the time it gave him to reflect and the opportunity for dreaming. He would swop matches which were forbidden for model cars.

20

His desk was filled with little objects which he would sell or exchange. And always in one pocket he would have a small car. He didn't want to be a farmer any more, as he had during the time at Wallenbuch, and drive a tractor; now he was completely taken up with motor cars — more and more with cars.

In winter, soup and buns were provided by the school so that the children didn't have to go home at midday and get themselves soaked to the skin. In the evening Seppi would come back with his pockets full of bread and potatoes which had been left over.

At the end of December 1943 Seppi became gravely ill. His mother was afraid that he had got diphtheria. The doctor reassured her and said that if it had been that he would already have been dead. His condition however got steadily worse. On the evening of the 31st December, almost out of his mind with worry and with Seppi almost unconscious, his father ran out into the street. In the Grand Place by sheer luck he ran into Doctor Perrier, a medical officer on leave, and begged him to come and see his son. It did not take long to make a diagnosis; Joseph was in the advanced stages of diphtheria. He would have to be taken to Berne immediately where they might be able to save him.

The long absence through illness, forty-three days in all, did nothing to improve his position at school. He finished his first year fourteenth out of a class of eighteen.

At eight, Seppi make his First Communion. Like all the other children he had a new suit and shoes for the occasion but, unlike the others, he did not show much enthusiasm for the effort, however modest, his parents had made.

'My old shoes were quite all right — I didn't need new ones. There were a lot of other things we needed more,' he told his astonished mother.

His third year at school he was taught by a master whose shouts and blows put him off lessons for good. More and

21

more reflective, he still sought the means to break out and find himself. But he did not forget his family. On Thursdays instead of playing with his chums, he would set off with his sisters and collect old paper which he would then sell. But it wasn't a haphazard affair; one by one' he went round the houses, the streets, the districts, following a plan which he had carefully worked out. The little barrow he pulled along was sometimes quite heavy — particularly when he had to hold it back on a hill. Fribourg is not exactly flat. The Varis or the Rue de la Grande Fontaine were almost precipitous. Then exhausted by the steep slope he would urge on his sister Marguerite who did not yet go to school to lend a hand and he would do his share. He meant to make some money — none of which Marguerite would ever see. He gave half to his mother but the other half he kept; it would go towards a bike. And he would clean the other boys' bicycles for a few sous or write out their lines for them.

When the daffodils were out, the whole family went and picked them on a Sunday. Seppi and his mother would then sell them. But in spite of all this Seppi had time to enjoy a normal childhood. After a run down the Poya riding on the back of a bob, he bought from a schoolfriend, Robert Boschung, a sledge mounted on wheels.

'It was one of my worst bargains ever,' he used to say.

The sun shone one Sunday in the summer and the Siffert family went to spend the day at Wallenbuch. Seppi was eleven. That afternoon he asked his father if he could drive the car. His father was interested to see how he would do; Seppi started off driving round the farm, changing gears — there was no synchromesh — without crashing them. His father couldn't believe it — how could he drive so well without ever having been taught?

The fact was that in a car Joseph didn't look at the view. The road and the way his father drove — very cleanly — was what fascinated him. He didn't look at anything else. His

22

highly developed powers of observation, his passion for cars and a natural ability were enough — he could drive straight off.

Intoxicated with pleasure he drove on and when at last he could bring himself to stop he brought the car gently to a standstill without stalling the engine. Proud of his son, Alois Siffert let him drive the car back to Fribourg. Keeping off the main roads, Joseph did not go very fast but he drove with assurance. His pleasure was damped a little later by his disappointment at the birth of a third sister, Theresa — he had so longed for a little brother. Disgusted, he could only spare a quick glance at the cradle.

On the 4th July 1948 Alois Siffert went to Berne for the Grand Prix of Europe on the Bremgarten Circuit and Joseph went with him. Like any boy of his age he was longing to go to a motor race and to see the great champions of the day — Farina, Villoresi, Wimille, Ascari, Chiron, Trossi, Sommer, Mays, de Graffenried, and so on.

An hour and a half before the start, as father and son were picnicking on a cold chicken which his mother had cooked for them, there was the sudden roar of an engine. It turned out that Sommer had got permission to do an extra practice lap before the race. Seppi dashed for the barrier and got there just as the Frenchman's Gordini appeared. Having watched him go past, he ran back to his father and — very impressed — shouted: 'He's gone, Papa, he was going very fast!'

From that moment Joseph never looked back. From his vantage point at Emyatt he took in the details of what he saw. Count Trossi won the race on an Alfetta at an average speed of over 90 mph; two drivers lost their lives — Achille Varzi was killed during practice on the Saturday and the Swiss Christian Kautz driving a Maserati was killed on the second lap of the race itself.

On the way home Seppi talked a lot; he told his father what had particularly struck him — Sommer's will to attack and how Raymond Mays on the ERA had always changed his gears at exactly the same point each time round.

When he got back to the house Joseph ran upstairs to his mother and told her: 'Mamma, on Sunday when I am grown up I shall go to Confession and Communion in the morning, and in the afternoon I shall drive a racing car.' Then he added, to make things quite clear, 'And I shall drive like Sommer; I shall attack.'

His parents didn't see any more in these statements than the dream of any small boy impressed by a new experience. But he didn't need a dream — his schoolboy dreams were over. He knew where he was going now. He had found his vocation and already he knew the risks of his chosen profession; he was going to be a racing driver. From now on Joseph Siffert wasn't going to dream any more, he was going to get down to realizing his chosen career.

Perhaps fortunately Seppi did not yet know all the problems that would confront him. However, one of them wasn't new, it was money. At this time it was not enough simply to have the sacred flame of motor racing enkindled within one; only well-off men had got anywhere — as witness Count Trossi, Prince Igor, Toulo de Graffenried, Harry Schell, Maurice Trintignant and numerous descendants of the great Italian families. So what? Joseph knew what he was going to to — become a driver of Grand Prix racing cars.

How was he going to do it? A 12-year-old schoolboy, son of a poor family? He didn't know yet; that didn't matter. The way might be difficult but now he knew the objective he would never let it out of his sight; his whole life would be directed to that end, whatever the sacrifice it might involve.

This pact with himself Joseph did not reveal to anyone, not even to his parents who naturally enough thought that the dream would fade as the child grew up. He spoke of it less and less. At school his chums would not take it seriously and nobody else cared. It was no good talking about it; he had to do something. He had to make some money. But there was still school.

In 1949 Joseph went on to the Secondary School. A better pupil now, he still didn't try very hard to make up for the time he had spent dreaming with Mademoiselle Huber. He preferred making copious notes on the track, the cars and the drivers. The mechanical side, however, didn't inspire him very much. But a good driver doesn't really have to be a first-class mechanic — the great drivers don't all know the secrets of their engines, far from it.

The most important thing at the moment was to get through school. A quiet, average sort of pupil, he rather kept out of the usual pranks. He didn't go in for brawling, but if his interests were at stake, he could be a very tough fighter. He really preferred dealing, and he always drove a hard bargain. On Saturday after school and on Sunday morning he would go round the town on foot bearing a sandwich board announcing the next match of the Fribourg football club. In fact, he had never been to a football match in his life but the five francs was very easily earned, like the little sums he picked up by selling to a cafe proprietor near the Cathedral the strong homebrewed drinks he bought around the countryside.

Joseph finished school at the end of the summer of 1951 and he wasn't very sorry to do so. But what was he going to do? He wanted to earn but he hadn't got a trade; an apprenticeship would take up too much time in his scheme of things and he was too much of an individualist to work for anyone but himself. So he decided to become a rag merchant. He already owned a bicycle good enough to equip with the maximum number of saddlebags.

After that, every fine morning Seppi would mount his cycle and comb the Fribourg area. His mother obviously did not approve of this activity which she refused to call a job but there was nothing to be done about it; Seppi had a hard head. Resigned, she would give him a hardboiled egg, some bread and a thermos of coffee for the day. Although he was mainly looking for wool or rabbit-skins, Seppi acquired anything on which he could make a little profit or which he thought might be useful.

This was how he came to bring his mother back a sewing machine one evening which he had bought for five francs. Another day, he gave his sister Adelaide a red coat which she wore for the next two years.

Working his way round the districts of Gruyere and Singine, mostly calling at the farms, Seppi got to know the character and mentality of the people he met pretty well. He soon realized that the country folk enjoyed a good grumble and he would encourage them to talk whilst he was weighing up the wool he was going to buy. He had his own way of weighing — one foot under the scales holding up a fair amount of the weight. He never bought the wool for less than 10 centimes a kilo but the ten or so kilos that he supported with his foot were well worth the effort involved!

In spite of bad weather, the long bicycle journeys, the disappointment when things went wrong and the plain boredom, the 15-year-old pressed on after his goal, still three years away. He carried on with courage and perseverance. His business didn't do badly. He was able to buy second-hand a small trailer which he hitched behind his bicycle. It meant that he could carry more and also avoid the risk of uncontrolled flight when the overloaded bike overbalanced. From time to time he would slip his mother twenty or fifty francs saying to her:

'Ah well, we poor devils must help each other.'

One day calling on a farmer in the Singine, Seppi saw a very nice tweed coat which looked as if it would fit him beautifully.

'It belongs to my son who has gone away for a couple of years,' the farmer told him when Joseph expressed interest.

'But in two years the coat will be all moth-eaten.'

'Oh no, I have filled the pockets with moth-balls,' said the farmer's wife.

'With moth-balls — you really think those little *poletz* [Fribourgeois for marbles] are mothproof? You must be joking!'

Joseph talked, argued and usually succeeded. His nose for a bargain, his cheek, let him try anything. 'I went so far that people were literally bowled over', he told me years later.

Finally the farmer agreed to let him put the coat on the scales. With a little help it registered just one kilo. Even Seppi hadn't the courage to offer just 10 centimes .for the coat. Hadn't they got some more bits and pieces, a few rags he could take off them? But a rag dealer had been there the week before and had taken all there was.

In the end Joseph departed with, neatly folded in the trailer, the coat for which he had paid ten centimes. He pedalled fast and hard not only because he enjoyed the speed but because he was terrified of being overtaken by the man with whom he had just done the deal! 'I never stole anything, but I always tried to buy everything at the lowest possible price,' he explained, with a great roar of laughter at the end of the story.

After a year Seppi worked out that although he had done quite well it wasn't going to be well enough to achieve his ends. The race track which he viewed with the same enthusiasm, seemed to get no nearer and an actual car seemed even further away. What was to be done? Sitting in a cafe one day, he overheard some soldiers talking at the next table.

'The exercises aren't too bad but what I can't stand is having to carry a great bag of empty cartridges cutting into your shoulders,' said one of them.

'That's no problem,' replied the other, 'all you have to do is bury the cases under a bank and come down empty.'

'Where do you do it?' Seppi broke in — already he had an idea. Empty cases could be sold for three francs eighty per kilo. And the next day he was off on his bicycle to the Lac Noir; from there he was going to climb on foot up the Riggisalp on the side of the Kaiseregg, a mountain which the military often used for shooting practice and manoeuvres.

He studied the ground like a gold-digger, occasionally scrabbling away a bit of ground hoping to find a cartridge-case. And suddenly he saw one, then two, then lots. He was delighted; as happy as a child which was all that he still was. Hurriedly he scooped them up — he didn't even know where to put them all. And there was still hundreds more. He didn't hesitate for long. He took off his trousers, tied up the ends and filled them with cases. Then bent double under the weight, he staggered down to the Lac Noir over 15,000 feet below.

He went back the next day and for days after that; he decided to specialize in the collection of cartridge cases. He consulted the papers for the announcement of shooting practice — they were really meant to warn the population to keep away from the areas where military exercises would be taking place. Seppi would install himself by a machinegun and offer the crew a couple of francs to let him collect the cases. Who could refuse a poor ragamuffin? At other times he would offer five francs to the grumbler with a full bag marching at the back of a column to empty it for him. Living with the soldiers like this he could do a lot of little jobs for them, and they would often say: 'Keep the money.' But it wasn't all fun and games: one day he found himself inadvertently right in the line of fire — terrified, he flattened himself to the ground on top of the cases which he had been so busy collecting. And in the evening, sometimes at night, he had to get back to Fribourg; to retrieve his bike he often had to go close to the farms and to the farmdogs.

But his operations prospered. He had not completely given up the rags and he certainly did not need to give up the hopes of a car. But to get there Joseph knew that he must have a job which would not only get over the last hurdle into racing but would provide something else — suppose he had to give up racing or had a serious accident early in his career? Joseph was well aware that he could not collect cartridge cases for the rest of his life and he did not want to remain a rag dealer. He wanted something to fall back on and for that he needed to learn a trade, even though he would earn less during the years of apprenticeship. To become a mechanic as his father had suggested was certainly a good idea, but mechanics rarely become racing drivers . . . What about a coachbuilder like Farina? In any case it had to be something to do with cars. The motor trade was one answer, and Joseph had already bought and sold more than one car, but the problem was to get hold of some numberplates. It is quite easy to drive without a licence, but it is much harder to manage without plates which in Switzerland are the personal property of the owner and not transferable with the car. The windfall from Pensier where a lady had asked Seppi to hand in her plates to the Canton Service des Automobiles — plates which he had been able to use for several months — was not likely to happen again.

Right in the middle of the old quarter of Fribourg, next door to the Central Prison, the Planche Barracks and the gasworks, the Frangi coachbuilding works had a reputation for good work and the high class of apprentice they turned out. Among them was Robert Boschung, his old schoolfriend.

On the morning of the 15th May 1952, Robert saw Seppi passing the barracks with his bicycle trailer loaded with rags.

'What are you up to?' the apprentice coach-builder asked.

'Door to door stuff,' replied Seppi. 'I buy and sell rags and scrap metal to make a bit of cash.'

'You don't want to learn a trade?'

'I haven't got the time, I must earn something.'

'An apprentice in this line of work can make a bit after his second year patching up and selling crashed cars. Frangi wants a new apprentice.'

'It's an idea — I'd like to talk to my father about it.'

That afternoon Seppi went to see Frangi and started work the next day. It's true that the pay was not tremendous — 40 centimes an hour and a 48-hour week for the first year. Joseph didn't make nearly as much as he had working for himself. But he liked the work; it brought him closer to cars. His employer was pleased with him: Seppi had ideas and character; he was not always very forthcoming but he learned quickly and worked hard. He seemed to be in his element. Apart from his work he always had something he was tinkering with. He knew a lot of people but he had few close chums and no friend whom he trusted with his secret. Even Yvette, who lived opposite the workshop and with whom Seppi was a little in love, did not know anything. But then, if he should fail, he didn't want anyone to know.

At home — the Siffert family was now living in the Schoenberg district on the Bellevue road — Seppi hardly talked about motors at all. His father had a little factory making lemonade. Seppi's sisters liked and admired him but they were also slightly in awe of him. It was perhaps because his strength of character, his determination and natural authority blended with his kindness and generous heart made a deep impression on them.

Two or three times a year Carlo Frangi gave a party to which he asked all his staff. He would also take the opportunity to check up on the education and behaviour of his apprentices; if they couldn't hold a fork or eat correctly, he would do something about it. Knowing this, the apprentice panelbeaters felt a personal link with their employer who was not only interested in teaching them a trade.

At seventeen, Seppi then in his second year as an apprentice, fitted up a small workshop at Bellevue where, in the evenings, he could repair cars on his own account and also do up crashed ones which he had started to buy to put right and sell. But the noise of the panelbeater's hammer in the small hours upset more than one neighbour. Frangi was soon informed by anonymous letters that his apprentice, Siffert, was taking on 'black' work. But to the chagrin of his not very courageous detractors, Seppi had already told his boss about his nocturnal activities. Knowing the financial difficulties of his apprentice's family, Frangi did not mind at all, particularly as Joseph carried out the work for him just as well as ever.

'Siffert wants to get somewhere,' his employer thought to himself: 'he has enough character and determination for me to leave him alone on his way.'

But the complaining neighbours were not going to admit defeat and they telephoned the police. The officers who came to investigate were amazed: 'You don't find a boy working as hard as this often enough to want to stop it,' they said to each other.

In the end a satisfactory arrangement was found — it was agreed that there would be no more hammering after 11 o'clock at night.

Normally a good pupil, Seppi did not always listen to what he was told and he had a few unfortunate experiences as a result. He was about to do some welding one morning, working very close to the canvas hood covering the cab of an aged Saurer truck; Frangi said that he had better take the hood off or he might set it alight.

'It'll be all right,' Seppi replied. 'I'll screen it off with some asbestos.'

'Well, if you do burn it, you'll have to pay for another.'

Seppi sniffed and started on the welding; and just as Frangi had predicted he burnt away part of the cab roof. The cost of the operation: 72 francs, which would be knocked off his salary — this was tough as he only made 20 francs a week. There it was — he just had to make the best of it. Years later, in October 1971, he met Frangi in Fribourg and the latter reminded him of the story.

'I could have killed you that morning,' Seppi told him, 'but I'd much rather have killed myself!'

This sharp lesson was just about the only unhappy recollection of Apprentice Siffert. There were many more of the funny stories, usually involving his friend Robert Boschung. One of them concerned a car, the brown paint-work of which had to be touched up after some repair work: Robert and Joseph tried to match the colour exactly but they simply couldn't get it right. Finally they bought a tin of shoe polish and painted that on — it was a much better match than any of their carefully prepared mixtures!

A willing and indefatigable worker, Joseph always liked to laugh and to enjoy himself after work or when the opportunity offered. But even now he had a near obsession with the idea that if a thing was worth doing, it was worth doing properly.

'Order and cleanliness,' he would say, 'cost very little and make the maximum impression.'

At the beginning of 1954, Seppi was driving alone one night without a licence or plates, heading towards Tavel in the Singine — the town of Tavel he avoided by going round a sideroad. However, just as he was about to re-join the main road he spotted a police car. Nervous of being picked up, the young man quickly backed into the woods, but rather imprudently he forgot to turn off his lights. The police car drove up and he embarked on a long story of how his father had just towed him there and that of course he had no intention of driving on the public road. Finally, after an hour of talking, of checking and cross-checking, during which Joseph managed not to contradict himself once, the patrol car drove off. Seppi was afraid that he would be given a very stiff fine even if his story was believed, which didn't seem very likely.

But he more or less got away with it — he was only fined the large sum of 14 francs.

The early days were not easy for Jo Siffert

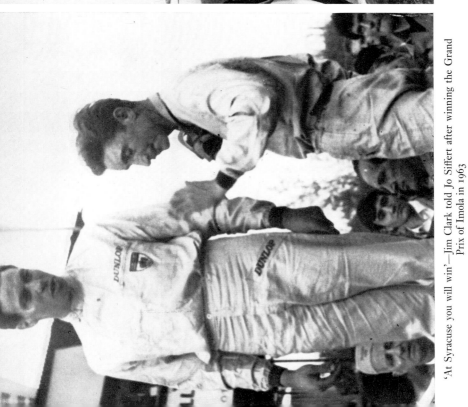

'At Syracuse you will win'—Jim Clark told Jo Siffert after winning the Grand Prix of Imola in 1963

At the wheel of the n
Lotus 20 at Chimay

The BRM-engined
Lotus 24 in the Mor
Grand Prix of 1964

Jo Siffert (Brabham
BRM) beating Jim (
(Lotus-Climax) at E
1965

On the 7th July, his eighteenth birthday, Jo Siffert went to the Bureau des Automobiles to apply for a provisional licence. Some of the officials expressed a certain surprise that he had not already got one, considering the number of times they had seen him driving; after looking through the dossier on the Tavel affair, they prescribed a period of suspension. Disgusted, Seppi went home but he carried on driving as before. On the day when he was finally able to take his test, he failed it through some bad parking.

Joseph was disappointed and also a little annoyed — after all, he had driven for a long time and never had an accident. But all this was soon forgotten with the Grand Prix of Berne in 1954 — which would be the last Grand Prix in Switzerland. Skipping the College of Arts and Engineering — he was doing a course there one day a week, actually in Berne — Joseph spent the whole weekend, just as he had every year since 1952, beside the Bremgarten track. Without any ticket or permit, he managed to get through the control and insinuate himself among the cars and drivers, watching, observing, noting everything. During practice and the race itself — which was won by Fangio — he stationed himself at various different points so that he could study the ideal line, see what happened when two or more drivers went through in a pack and compare the best of the drivers. He didn't go for those who played a waiting game; he liked the ones who pressed on. He cheered Ascari, taking Fangio on the inside on braking, and he was thrilled watching the duel between the two leading British drivers — Stirling Moss and Mike Hawthorn.

But before the Grand Prix there was a race for modified. sports cars; one driver, also from Fribourg and a former motor-cycle champion, particularly impressed Seppi with his handling of a 2-litre Maserati. His name was Benoit Musy, the son of the ex-Councillor, Jean-Marie Musy. Taking second place behind the unbeatable Daetwyler, he drove a fantastic race. That night, thinking over his wonderful weekend, Seppi told himself that one day he would wear a similar helmet to Benoit Musy: red, with three white bands and a Swiss cross on the front.

He got his driving licence at last on the 14th September. It was an important step because it meant he could intensify his commercial activities. He bought a car which he was going to keep for himself — his first car. It was a Peugeot 202 which he acquired from Jean Ballaman, the brother of the great footballer and captain of the Swiss team. Joseph was very proud driving around in a car registered in his own name. Sometimes at lunchtime he would drive his boss home, or he would lend the car to his father for the afternoon.

'Usually when he is eighteen a young man borrows his father's car, but with me it was the other way round,' he would tell me later.

One evening, Joseph telephoned his mother to tell her that he had damaged the car — he had run out of road and crashed into a henhouse between Guin and Fribourg. He didn't want his father to know; he was nervous of him. Strict, Alois Siffert didn't like too much joking and didn't approve of his son going out every night. He was quite likely to lock the front door — but Joseph had his accomplices: his sisters. Marguerite would often leave a window open for him or even risk going down and opening the door.

During the winter, when his father was in charge of the skating rink in the Jura district, his nights out were a bit different. He was allowed out, but only to hose down the ice. When he had finished his panel-beating, he would join his father and run water carefully over the rink, regulating the flow with their thumbs.

'The whole of that winter I never got more than four hours' sleep every night, because I had to be punctual the next morning at the coachworks,' he told me once as we were driving across France.

34

Urged on by Robert Boschung who encouraged him to put a bigger effort into sport, he joined the CP ice hockey team — CP stood for the Club des Patineurs — of which Jean Claude Fontana, the young photographer, was also a member. Playing in the second side, he played in his first match at Morat. Seppi didn't know any of the rules, he just improvised, hanging around the opposite goalpost in the hopes of scoring a few quick points. The result was unequivocal; Morat won by 8 points to 1. Seppi decided that perhaps he was not made for team games. Was he too much of an egotist? Not really, but for each situation, he would put up an answer and then try it.

If car racing was his ultimate target, any motorised sport interested him. Terribly tempted by a second-hand Rumi motor-cycle, he succumbed and took out a motor-cycle licence on the 6th June 1955.

Motor cycling became a real passion; even on ordinary roads he would ride as if he was in a race, on the limit. The pleasure that Seppi obviously took in the Rumi and its handling amazed Robert Boschung, who was his closest friend at this time. Motor cycling seemed to come to him as a second nature, and yet his friends had not even suspected that it existed.

At home his mother couldn't help fussing a little, just as she couldn't help noticing traces of blood where his trousers had been oddly ripped. But what could she do? She knew her son and she knew he was working towards something which he did not want given away yet.

In fact, the speed and danger had so intoxicated him that Seppi thought he would try his hand at motor cycle competition work. A number of world champion Grand Prix drivers had started on motorbikes — among them Benoit Musy. Full of enthusiasm, Joseph made up his mind and told his parents about his ideas: 'If you bring a racing bike into the house, I'll find a rock and smash it up,' his father

35

said — although he didn't really take what Seppi was saying any more seriously than he had after the Grand Prix of Berne in 1948.

Joseph decided then that he would say nothing more about it.

In his twentieth year, Siffert was the oldest of Frangi's apprentices; Boschung had just finished and set up on his own. Joseph was actually lodging with Auguste Stritt in Tavel who had been advised not to get too mixed up with the young Siffert because his business affairs, if they were not actually dubious, were certainly obscure. As far as his affairs were concerned, Seppi was certainly not going to bang on about them over cafe tables, but they were doing quite all right.

His apprenticeship nearly over, Siffert had nothing more to learn in the field of coachbuilding. The theories which he had been able to learn, he had been able to put into practice over a considerable period. His business, buying crashed cars and doing them up for re-sale, had done well. On Saturdays, his little sister Theresa polished and cleaned up the cars which he would sell during the week, inside and out for one franc. At nine years old that was enough. Thinking that the service wasn't worth as much, she refused her first pay-packet, but when the service soon became a regular thing, she made enough pocket money to become the envy of her friends.

On the 18th May, 1956, Joseph Siffert passed his final exams as a coachbuilder with flying colours. One more stage had been passed. He had a profession. His future was assured. But the race hadn't yet started because he had to do his military service. Seppi, the individualist, didn't look forward to becoming, for four months, Recruit Siffert. But anyway he could get over that — he would have to take the good with the bad. For the moment, he was twenty. He had a craft and a target. Was he not quite fortunate?

His hair cut short, a small suitcase in his hand, Recruit

Siffert arrived at Bulach Barracks in the Canton of Zurich on the 23rd July 1956 as a mechanic in the Transport Service, to which he had managed to get himself posted. The military life did not seem to please him any more than his room-mates, and from the beginning the weakness in his leg and right foot, now that he was wearing heavy boots, gave him trouble and prevented him running. Even when he had been collecting cartridges on the slopes of the Kaiseregg he had never worn anything but ordinary walking shoes. After a fortnight, when his mother, sisters and Yvette met him at the station for his first leave, he was limping badly.

Next week the doctor at the training school recommended his discharge. However, his company commander, who had noticed the ease with which he switched from one vehicle to another — Joseph had only got his licence to drive heavy vehicles four days before his call-up — and his general understanding of motor transport, did not want to lose such a valuable recruit. Joseph himself did not really want to stay; he had tried it out and decided that he didn't like it and didn't want any more. After telephoning his parents, the captain suggested a special routine — no marching, no boots, and permanent attachment to the transport section.

'I go through the training school the same as the others, or I'm off,' Seppi said. And on the 15th August he went back to Fribourg for good.

There was no shortage of work. Relieved of his training and military service, Joseph was going to be able to work up his second-hand car business. He also wanted to get hold of Michel Piller — the racing motor-cyclist from Fribourg whom he had watched several times racing at Bienne — because he wanted to have a go himself on a grass track.

CHAPTER TWO

At this time, in 1956, Michel Piller was running a Gilera 125 cc. A professional mechanic, he had a small motor cycle business at the top of the Rue du Varis; he was perfectly happy simply preparing motor cycles for races and enjoying his hobby.

Michel soon became a close friend of the young Joseph Siffert, five years his junior, who had already told him that he wanted to race himself. Before giving him any encouragement — for really how can you advise a beginner without cash and with no resources except his two hands and his training as a coachbuilder to take up motor sport for a living? — Michel decided to watch Seppi in action. And so it was that the two men agreed to go on a trip together to Romont, Seppi on his Rumi and Michel riding another machine. The experience was conclusive: Piller knew at once that his young friend was extremely gifted; the way he set up a corner was something exceptional, the more so as he seemed to understand perfectly that such mastery could only be a gift. Seppi rode like an expert and this although he had no practical experience and no-one had ever told him how to ride. His only apparent fault was to go flat out without taking sufficient account of the revs which he was exacting from the engine of his Rumi.

The test run of nearly twenty miles from Fribourg to Romont soon became a habit; every morning at 5 o'clock they would meet for the morning jaunt — a run that was a jaunt in name only.

With his growing passion for motor sport Siffert was absolutely convinced that he was taking the right course but the principle remained — how could he go on without making a lot of money? There were two alternatives open to him: he could open a bodywork repair shop — which would need money; or he could get work in one — which would neither bring him in very much nor leave him with much free time. Joseph found an escape route. He would set off sailing along on his motorbike roaming over the Suisse Romande and part of German Switzerland, touring all the garages looking out for one or several crashed cars which he could do up on the spot and just generally keeping his eyes open. He only bought a minimum of equipment and borrowed the rest from wherever he was. This style of operation brought him into contact with a large number of garage owners some of whom wished to get rid of one or two old bangers and others who wanted a bargain to offer a client. Joseph acted as middleman.

He soon bought more than he could cope with. At Granges-Paccot where his family lived on the edge of Fribourg, a friend and neighbour, Jean-Paul Thiemard, took on a few that Seppi brought in. His mother cleaned them inside and out. The whole business was not popular with Alois Siffert who would have preferred his son to have got a more regular job. To achieve this he thought that Seppi ought to leave Fribourg for a bit. An old friend from his military days was quite happy to employ Joseph at his garage in Saint Gallen. He could also put him up, but the distance from his house to the garage would mean buying a motor cycle and he knew that the Siffert family was not well off. 'If he knew that Seppi had been riding around on a bike for a long time,' Seppi's father said to himself; but he had already decided that the idea wasn't worth trying. Seppi had gone too far.

However, relations were not always of the best and some discussions between Seppi and his father led to high feelings and raised voices. The day after one such altercation Seppi had to go to Monza where he was going to take part, with Michel Piller, in a motor cycle race. Joseph did not dare tell his father. In the end it was not until he was about to leave that he told him the object of the trip. Alois Siffert was so angry that Seppi decided not to return to his home. He set himself up at Villarepos in a little workshop where he could both live and work. His friend, Jean-Paul Thiemard, moved in with him. His mother and sisters visited the exile frequently, often bringing something to stock up the little trellised food store which he had installed in the workshop.

At the start of the 1957 season Seppi and Michel Piller decided to race together: Joseph swapped a damaged car for a Gilera 125 which Michel had ridden the year before. The first thing to do was to get Seppi a racing licence; for this purpose Seppi took part in several grass track races, though he did not really enjoy them, and most of the hill-climbs taking place in Switzerland. Spare parts being almost non-existent, he had to do a good bit of improvising. For one race he borrowed a bike from Gaby Guisolan, another Fribourgeois who spent his spare time motor cycle racing. Through bad luck and inexperience, Seppi burned out the valves which earned him a major rocket.

'Nobody goes in for a motor cycle race if they don't know how to ride. You must be mad to overstretch an engine like that. You won't get anywhere by massacring the machinery,' yelled Gaby.

'It wasn't my fault. The head came unscrewed and seized the valves,' replied Seppi, although he was not very proud of himself.

With his new racing licence in his pocket Joseph decided to enter for several international races with Michel. Seppi was back at Granges-Paccot on Christmas Eve 1957 and things were beginning to take shape. He had made enough money to be able to afford a more powerful motorbike, an AJS 350, new, which arrived unassembled but which Michel soon put together although he pointed out that a vital part was missing.

'That doesn't matter — when we get there we will surely find someone who can help,' Seppi said.

The day before they left for the Norisring where Seppi would compete in his first international epreuve and his first race on a 350 cc machine, his father noticed the bike in the garage at Granges-Paccot.

'Who does this death machine belong to?' he enquired.

'It's not mine; a friend in Geneva has lent it to me to do one race,' Seppi replied, fearing the worst for his enterprise.

Fortunately the discussion stopped there. But the next day just after Seppi had left for the Norisring, his mother told her husband that it wouldn't be Seppi's only race on that bike because it actually was his.

In Germany on the autobahn leading to the Norisring Seppi longed to try out his AJS; he told Michel that he must have a go — that the missing part, although doubtless important, was not essential. They stopped and unloaded the bicycle. Seppi straddled her and thundered off. Michel got back in the car and, a few miles further on, stopped to pick up Seppi and put the bike back in again; then they pressed on for Nuremberg once again.

Practice started as soon as they got to the circuit. Seppi went off at full speed, took some crazy chances and turned in fourth best time in front of the works riders. Already he had been lucky: it had been raining on and off and a pool of water in one of the bends had not completely dried out. Unfortunately the puddle lay right across the correct line for the corner and all the riders lost several tenths of a second avoiding it. All except Siffert — who rode right through it. An English competitor remarked on his recklessness and added that it was not worth the risk anyway because the race didn't count for the world championship. Joseph accepted the remark but not the rider — an epreuve was above all a race, whether it counted for the world championship or not. Siffert's times were so good that the organizers were asked to check on the cylinder capacity of the unknown Swiss' motor cycle. There wasn't time for a proper check so they made Siffert sign a document confirming that his bike conformed with the regulations.

For the race Joseph was on the front row. Small, thin and slightly built, he wondered if he had enough strength to push the bicycle fast enough so that it would keep going when he let the clutch out in first gear — the compression was very high. But anyway he would soon see!

He made a bad start; Seppi turned on the petrol a bit late, lost some time and also his place among the leading group. But he was in the saddle. After several laps of hard riding it began to rain. That's lucky, Joseph thought, they'll reduce the pace a bit and I shall be able to get up with the leaders again. Two riders came off in front of him but nothing could put him off. He was in a race and, whether it rained or not, he was going to make a go of it. But his impetuosity led him to overdo things: going into a bend Seppi slithered and crashed onto the track. He didn't let go of his machine, however, which came to a standstill and then, the petrol cap having been ripped off, caught fire. Joseph let go and rolled into the grass. By a miracle he wasn't hurt — what did really hurt him was watching his motor cycle burning. Luckily the safety service worked well and the blaze was soon extinguished: only the tyres and the rubber parts were all melted — the rest was repairable.

It all made quite an impression in the world of motor cycling and the organizers of the race wanted to sign Siffert up for the next races. Seppi accepted for the lot, saying loftily of course he had another machine. In fact he would have to work very hard to restore the only one he possessed. But that didn't matter — what was essential was to have something to work for.

On his return to Fribourg Joseph didn't know quite how to tackle his father. Then he remembered a newspaper cutting with a photo of one of the runners. 'Look, Papa, it's Lorenzetti the world champion. He only got fifth best time in practice and started on the second row . . . behind me . . . !

But Alois Siffert was already fully informed. The head of the Service des Automobiles, Monsieur Crotti, had met him, told him the whole story and congratulated him warmly!

The repairs did not take quite as long as he had thought; the engine was intact. The most laborious task was the final re-polishing of the wheel rims and spokes. His bike might not be the fastest or the most up-to-date but it would always be the best turned-out. Yvette, whose job it was to make the spokes gleam with scraps of carbon, knew something about this too.

The motor bike was ready in time for the race on the Sachsenring, near Leipzig, the start of a long series that Michel and Joseph would contest in the eastern part of Germany, a series which would give Seppi plenty of experience but would do nothing to rob him of his youthful impetuosity.

At the Sachsenring, Seppi fought a long duel for fifth place with a German runner racing on the limit and covering over 30 yards on one wheel after he had touched the straw bales. At the end, he climbed off his bike and fell flat on the ground; his legs just couldn't support him, he could hardly speak. He hadn't worried about it in the heat of the contest, but his chin had been continually hitting the fuel tank because the padding there had been torn off. For two days Joseph couldn't chew anything and his teeth felt as if they had been partly extracted. But these troubles did not stop him giving the German rider a run for his money. On a works bike he had had to take unheard-of risks to beat the Swiss independent.

Looking back on the period Seppi admitted his early impetuosity, but he would explain: 'I was mad then; I would go flat out from the start, no matter what. It wasn't just a race to me, this was my one chance to get there and so many drivers didn't make it. It's no good starting gently if you want to be taken seriously, to make a name. You have to be tough as a beginner so that you can calm down later, be able to calm down and keep going. When a beginner is killed, people say he was mad, but it's not really true — he was only playing double or quits!'

Seppi was taking considerable risks. The works bikes were definitely faster in terms of sheer speed; he could only compete with them when the going was difficult and the rider could make a difference. In one round-the-houses race through a town Seppi came out of one corner, every time round, with both his wheels running in the angle between the edge of the pavement and the road. The step of the cycle and the edge of his boot were so polished by this treatment that they fairly shone. There were lessons in all these races — and he did not need to be taught anything twice. Michel, to whom Seppi had confided his secret ambition to become a racing driver, understood his impetuous friend and the forces which drove him.

Piller could not go to every meeting with Seppi and then the latter would find somebody else to accompany him. For Locarno it was Fredy Haenni who came to help; however, when they left Fribourg they had laid the bike down the wrong way and the oil from the gearbox leaked back onto the clutch and this had to be changed in double quick time. But Seppi always managed to fix things and if he could not get round trouble, he would at least make it manageable; little problems were rapidly and positively resolved. For some time whenever he started up the motor bike engine at

Granges-Paccot, a neighbour complained about the noise and the police would come round, even if it was in the middle of the day. The objector seemed to be a special agent who, by chance, shared a party line with the Siffert family. All Seppi had to do when he had to test his motorbike after the next race was to take their receiver off the hook and the other telephone would not work; and it succeeded — this time the police did not call!

When he agreed to go with Seppi to Zwevezeele near Bruges, Pierre Gross thought he was just taking a little trip to Belgium with no trouble. He did not think he was embarking on three unforgettable days. They were supposed to leave at 11 o'clock but Seppi told Pierre that he had just sold the car in which they had intended to travel to Belgium; and the motorbike was still in bits as Michel and Fredy had not yet finished assembling it. 'It doesn't matter,' said Seppi, 'I've got a Mercedes.'

It was actually an old banger which Robert Boschung had opened up at the back, and he had also cut away part of the roof so that the bike could travel upright — the lesson of Locarno had not been forgotten. It was quite a good answer if the draught had not been increased by fixing a tarpaulin over the back.

At 8 that evening, the equipage was finally ready. A quick snack and the two entrants set off for Basle. On the road Seppi stopped at every breaker's yard and every second-hand car dealer: he wanted a back door for the Peugeot 403 which he had taken in exchange for the car he had sold that morning. After crossing the frontier Seppi handed the driving over to Pierre, rolled up in his sleeping bag and went to sleep. One of the secrets of his powers of complete and rapid recuperation lay in his ability to get to sleep regardless of the noise or the surroundings. About 5 o'clock on the autumn morning, the chopped-off Mercedes arrived at the Luxembourg frontier where the Customs men did not seem anxious to do anything about them in a hurry. Seppi hopped out, lifted the barrier and told Pierre to drive on! At this, the Customs men rushed out of their shed and Seppi gave them tremendous stick, complaining that he was having to do their work for them in raising the barrier.

Having got to the town of Luxembourg the two men stopped at the station buffet and had some breakfast. When it came to pay the bill, Seppi asked Pierre: 'Have you got any money?'

'Yes — 30 Swiss francs. What about you?'

'I've got 40 francs — but they're Swiss too!'

The waitress finally settled for the Swiss money after Seppi, a little tetchy that morning, had told her to take it or leave it!

When they got to the circuit the 50 cc class practice had already started and, as they had to cross the track to get to the pits, they had to wait — or rather they would have had to wait if Seppi had not told Pierre to shift the straw bales and then charged across the track barely giving Pierre time to hang on to the back of the car.

And so the equipage arrived at the paddock escorted by a crowd of tiny motorcycles, the riders of which wanted to know what the hell a chopped-off Mercedes was doing on the track during practice. The official reception was unenthusiastic and ended with a magisterial ticking-off. Joseph didn't worry. He had got there and that was what mattered to him. He carried on unloading his motorbike in silence.

It wasn't a world championship meeting but as there wasn't anything else that weekend, all the elite had turned up — in particular the English contingent with among others Bob Crown, Bob Anderson and one of the Hilton brothers. At the end of the practice Seppi had fourth best time, just as at the Norisring, which put him on the front row. But this was not very much to the liking of the experienced riders — they told him he was taking too many chances and

46

with his habit of passing them on bends he was forcing them to take risks too. Siffert didn't care: all that mattered was the result.

The practice was followed by one for the 500 cc machines. Seppi hadn't actually got a bigger bike but he was entered for both races. As you can't tell a 350 from a 500 from the outside, all that was needed was a few strokes of a paintbrush. The 350s had white numbers on a black ground, and the 500s black on yellow ground. He didn't bother with hammers and screwdrivers which he could always borrow, he simply brought a little pot of paint which enabled him to have an extra go if the engine held out. But during the second practice the engine blew up — it was finished. Siffert couldn't race and he couldn't even collect his starting money. Without any cash, how were they going to get back? They could do without food — it wouldn't be for the first time — but the car couldn't do without petrol.

That night Seppi and Gross didn't know where they were going to sleep. It was terribly cold in their half-open car. They went to a cafe and stayed there till closing time, the moment of truth. Then they told the patron of their sad plight and he offered them a bed — but without any bedclothes. It was a great deal better than nothing, but it was far too cold to sleep. They ended up by taking down the curtains in the passage and wrapping themselves up in those.

On Sunday things looked brighter; Siffert managed to persuade the organizers to give him a small payment which would get them back to Switzerland. For the race he took on a job as time-keeper for a German competitor running an NSU 250 but neither Joseph nor Pierre had the correct arm-band for this function. A policeman approached Pierre who tried to explain but got pushed into a little gulley by the track — he jumped over the stream at the bottom and climbed out on the other side. The officer then turned to Seppi; before the policeman could say a word, the Swiss lashed out and knocked him into the ditch. The crowd in the stands opposite fairly howled with laughter. Joseph then dropped his board and ran back to the car, all set to go. But it was quickly surrounded by police who wanted to see his papers.

'Give them your fishing licence if you've got it, but for goodness' sake don't give them your passport,' advised Pierre Gross. Siffert made the grave mistake of handing over his racing permit to the police who, tired of being a public laughing-stock, went off. Siffert had to get his licence back because he was due to race at Bilbao the next weekend. He found the policeman again, who turned out to be the chief of police for the area, and he was told to come back to their headquarters. This had been set up for the occasion in the rehearsal room of the Municipal Band.

Flanked by two solid constables, Siffert and Gross had to wait whilst the superintendent made out his report. When it was given to him to sign Joseph saw that it was written in Flemish and he tore it up. The policeman started all over again. In the end, when everyone had calmed down a bit, the Race Director managed to sort it all out satisfactorily.

Impulsive and sometimes hasty, Siffert always wanted to get to the heart of things, to take full responsibility himself. He had a quick intelligence and a spontaneity which sometimes got him into youthful scrapes, but he always learned his lessons and incidents, although painful at the time, would become happy memories. Throughout all these early vicissitudes, his courage and determination stood him in good stead and enabled him always to find a solution.

Towards the end of the 1958 season, Edgar Strub, the motor cycle combination rider, was looking for a passenger — not easy to find because racing on a sidecar is dangerous and entails a great deal of responsibility without any mechanical interest. Three Swiss had become world famous in this class of racing — two men on three wheels: Fritz

Concentration before the start: Nurburgring 1963

The Cooper-Maserati in the Mexican Grand Prix of 1966

Jo Siffert tries a Formula Two Ferrari at Modena

Scheidegger, Florian Camathias and Edgar Strub. What encouraged Strub to get in touch with the young Siffert was the fact that his courage and determination were recognized throughout the world of motor cycle racing.

'Certainly, I am entirely at your service,' Seppi told him on the telephone.

Sidecar races were normally held before or after races reserved for solo motor cycles, so Siffert normally found himself racing twice on one day — with the 350 motorbike and on the sidecar.

The Strub and Siffert partnership soon made the headlines when they competed in and won their first race up in Helsinki. From there they went to Sweden. Seppi soon learned how to operate as a passenger: his sense of balance, his enjoyment of risk and his love of speed were just what was wanted. Scheidegger confirmed this; he said that Seppi would lean so far out of the sidecar that Strub was sometimes pushed to squeeze past the other competitors.

Conditions during their Finnish trip were only just bearable: Strub had very little money and Siffert had practically none at all. It was terribly cold in Finland and it had started to snow. The soles of Seppi's shoes had worn through but he simply cut out some pieces of cardboard and stuck them inside.

At the end of the 1958 season, Strub and Siffert decided to intensify their effort for the coming year, though Seppi still gave precedence to his motor bike and concentrated first of all on the Swiss Championship which he had hopes of winning. Michel Piller always raced in the 125 category but Joseph now decided to change his AJS 350 for a Norton which had belonged to Strub and for which he would pay by working in Strub's garage at Starrkirch, near Olten.

The season began well in both categories. Siffert did not always return to Fribourg between races; the work for Strub became a regular arrangement and Joseph did a good deal of repair work on old cars there. His job as a sidecar rider provided less to maintain the man than his work as a coachbuilder — particularly a coachbuilder as good as Seppi. 'He was not only the nicest man, but also the best coachbuilder I have ever known,' Edgar Strub later declared.

A strong friendship grew up between Joseph and Edgar, who when he came to Fribourg would always bring marzipan for the little Theresa; Edgar was one of the few who knew about Seppi's plans to get into motor racing. For the time being, though, Seppi made a name as a sidecar rider and, with his strong personality, became the leader of the Swiss contingent. Scheidegger particularly admired his tenacity; Seppi would never admit defeat. And his courage would spread to close runners whom he would sometimes even lecture in mid-race.

'Either you are a pair of chumps or I'm a genius,' he said one day to Scheidegger and Camathias, just after he had beaten them, 'but as I'm no more of a genius than you, you must be a pair of chumps!'

Siffert threw himself into every race, body and soul, but he had a horror of underhand methods: there were enough built-in risks without the competitors trying to foul each other up. One day during practice one pair who had the sidecar on the right of the motorbike got badly in Strub's way — his sidecar was on the left — as he was overtaking. Annoyed, Joseph decided to teach them a lesson; the next time round, at over 90 mph, he administered from his sidecar a smart kick in the pants to the unsporting rider in the other sidecar.

They didn't win all their races, and they certainly had a few moments of drama. One of these came during practice. Siffert slipped up and caught his left hand in the wheel of the sidecar, tearing all his fingernails badly. At the dressing station after they had bandaged him up they told him not to race the next day. 'That's what you think,' said Seppi. 'I've got to do some motorbike practice this afternoon!'

And he did. He could hardly work his clutch with his injuries and he fell off. By good luck he wasn't hurt — or rather wasn't hurt any more. But the motorbike was damaged and he could not repair it in time for the 350 race.

The sidecar race was tough. Seppi could only use one hand for the whole series of manoeuvres which had to be carried out. Then the bandage came off his left hand. This would not have mattered much if the overfilled left carburettor of the BMW 500 combination hadn't spilled itself over his wounds. Suddenly it was near disaster. Handicapped by his injury, Joseph slipped as they were cornering and fell out of the sidecar. He just managed to hang on with his right hand and, at 115 mph, he was dragged along the track. It was a superhuman effort and he almost let go. Crouched over the handlebars, Strub, his eye on the right edge of the track, saw nothing. He braked slightly for the next corner, and then Seppi found himself thrown back into the sidecar. It was a double bend, a left followed by a right. If he didn't hang on, they wouldn't make it — they would just go straight on down the escape road. Forgetting the pain, Joseph hung out as if nothing had happened, but the race wasn't over, he just had to keep concentrating to the end.

Strub had no idea of what had happened until he had crossed the line. He was horrified: Seppi had no boots — a spectator brought them to the pits after the race; his backside and knees were covered in blood and he had no toenails left. The nurses who dealt with him were amazed: 'If we clean all this in antiseptic it will be quite all right,' they told Seppi, who could hardly walk except on his heels and certainly could not get into a pair of shoes. He would have to treat himself to a pair of high-lacing boxers' boots.

'I couldn't have borne it,' Seppi told me long afterwards, 'but after I had got myself back into the sidecar I saw the double bend and I knew that my life and Strub's depended on the way I hung out — I forgot all about my fall. As for the rest of the race, it certainly hurt like the devil, but I could bear it when we got to the end!'

Racing was the supreme objective of Joseph Siffert's life and the realization of that end justified all his sacrifices. The hardships he had endured had not only taught him to know himself better, but in particular to know his limitations and how to conquer them by willpower and determination.

The Tourist Trophy race held every year in the Isle of Man was one of the toughest races there is and also the most murderous; some 40 miles long, the circuit takes in a formidable number of bends, most of them over or round such bumps that the bikes take off into the air completely.

Siffert and Strub decided to have a go at it. Joseph had never crossed the Channel and couldn't speak a word of English; and the same went for Strub.

They did the trip in a Chevrolet which Seppi had bought in Bumplitz near Berne for 300 francs; the chap who had sold it to him had said that it couldn't do more than 30 mph. The two men loaded aboard the sidecar and the two motor cycles — Strub's Norton and Siffert's AJS.

When they got to London they were spotted by a group of enthusiasts all mounted on very big motor bikes. Joseph soon got the message over: they were on their way to the Isle of Man but first they were going to have to get across this enormous unknown city . . . The fans, the first he had picked up in England, cleared a route for him with hooters and sirens blaring — and at a rather rapid pace for someone who had never driven on the left of the road before. They had hardly got to the circuit when the two Swiss were surprised and rather shaken to meet a hearse: practice had already been going on for some time and two riders had been killed.

The formalities completed, the bikes unloaded, Joseph launched out on the extremely difficult circuit on which he would have to qualify before he could start in the race. The circuit, however, was so long and so difficult that it was impossible to memorise in two or three days. Seppi lost two boots brushing a rock and a wall. One of them belonged to Michel Piller who long afterwards asked for it back. Seppi roared with laughter and christened him 'Me Old Boot.'

Although he managed to qualify, Seppi soon went out of the race with mechanical trouble. The sidecar race went better and they finished up in seventh place.

Living like gipsies, with two small monkeys as companions, waving from their racing helmets hung at the back of the car, Edgar Strub and Joseph Siffert toured Europe. 1959 was a year of success. The partnership won at Bourg-en-Bresse, at La Faucille, at the Col de Malval, at Zandvoort in Holland, at Zeltweg in Austria, at Madrid, in the Grand Prix of the Saarland, at Vesoul and they finished with a third place in the General Classification of the motor cycle combinations world championship.

The motor cycle results were also good; Siffert won enough national events to get quite easily the Swiss 350 cc Championship. Michel Piller also did well and won the same title in the 125 cc class.

Full of excitement, the year 1959 also enabled Seppi to put by a little capital which he would certainly need if only to pay for the valves he bent, due to his total inability to keep a weather eye on the rev counter of his Norton.

At one hill-climb, Chatel-St-Denis — Les Paccots, in the Canton of Fribourg, Joseph had Fredy Haenni as his assistant. Half an hour before the start, he wandered off leaving Fredy to warm up the machine, and didn't come back. Worried, the mechanic sent off his wife to look for him. She found Seppi two or three hundred yards away, sitting propped up against a tree and fast asleep — in spite of the 250 cc bikes which were making their climbs! As soon as he had woken up, Joseph went out and set up a new record for the climb!

Sleep was always as vital a factor as concentration to Siffert. It didn't matter when or where or for how long — sleep was for him not just rest but his only way of setting aside, perhaps only for an instant, his many cares.

By the end of the 1959 season Joseph Siffert's name was recognised throughout the world of motor cycle and combination racing. The Swiss was no longer a beginner: there was a real hope that the next year he would begin to matter.

And this was the moment when he decided to quit motor cycles; he had saved up enough to be able to move from two to four wheels. He would have to start again; all the doing without food and the endless financial problem. It seemed very bitter not to follow his vocation in motor cycle racing just when everything seemed to have become easy!

His friends were horrified to see him give up his Norton for something so speculative, among them Gaby Guisolan. He saw the point later: 'Seppi was always two years ahead of us,' he said.

CHAPTER THREE

On the 13th February 1960 Joseph Siffert took part in his first event for motor cars — an ice slalom organized on the Lac Noir by the Fribourg section of the Swiss Automobile Club. Seppi drove a Jaguar, much too heavy to slip rapidly round the markers laid out on the frozen lake. The result was distinctly unflattering: Joseph was classified 34th out of 35 runners with a time of 3 minutes 57.3 seconds. The best time was put up by Jean-Louis Etter on a Lancia with 2 minutes 46 seconds.

The Swiss motor cycle champion didn't worry too much; his next objective was to get hold of a competition licence for cars and to get himself a racing car.

In 1955 after the tragic accident at Le Mans, the opponents of motor sport had launched a virulent campaign to shut down all circuit racing in Switzerland, and in particular to stop the Swiss Grand Prix which was held every year at Berne on the Bremgarten circuit. Unfortunately, they succeeded and the ban, still in force today, was written into the new Road Traffic Act of 1958. As a result of this all driving events organized by the Swiss Automobile Club — the ACS — have to be staged abroad, mostly at Monza, the Nurburgring and Montlhery.

Siffert turned up next in the spring of 1960 at Montlhery with a blue Alfa Tiger 1600, accompanied by Yvette and Michel Piller who had now given up all his sporting activities to become Seppi's Number One. Attentive to the theory of the thing, Siffert was conspicuous for the unorthodox way he put into practice — or rather did not apply at all — the basic principles he was being taught. Cutting down his braking distances to the bone, he would charge into each bend on the brink, completely obscuring the correct line. On top of this, his habit of taking the other novices on the inside going into a corner seemed to be already an obsession with him and did not go down at all well with the track marshals.

Joseph tried hard to make them understand that his theory was certainly correct for a driver running solo and he knew that it wasn't the answer when a tight bunch of drivers were leading a race and the last man to brake goes into the corner first and must set up the ideal line. It was no good. Aspirant Siffert earned himself several black marks.

Simultaneously with his launching out into racing driving, Seppi hotted up his second-hand car business. He did rather less panel-beating, and instead preferred now to act as intermediary, mainly for the Geneva and German-Swiss motor trade. In Geneva he came across Lucien Balsiger again when he sold him a car that he had bought the day before in Fribourg from Leon Kolly who was running the Bear Cafe. Balsiger had a garage in the Rue du Cendrier and later at No. 64 Rue de Montoux. At that time he had on his books a Formula Junior Fiat-Stanguellini which Seppi had seen running at Aix-les-Bains, the day when a footbridge had collapsed onto the track during a race. Joseph would very much have liked to buy the Stanguellini but he kept right off the subject, appearing to be quite uninterested, until Bisule actually suggested the idea to him.

In May the two men met up to go to the Monaco Grand Prix. On the way Bisule tried to sell him the idea, but Seppi didn't seem that keen, saying that he couldn't make up his mind between buying a new bike or this second-hand car. In fact, he was longing to buy the Stanguellini but only at the best price! After the Formula One practice the two Swiss decided to walk around the circuit. At Ste Devote they agreed a price and shook hands on it: 'Worth all the documents in the world!' Bisule would say.

On the 11th June 1960 Joseph Siffert and Michel Piller went to Geneva to collect the Stanguellini — a Formula Junior Modena car with rigid axles and a blown Fiat 1100 engine. The car wasn't very competitive and the oil temperature gauge rose nearly as rapidly as the rev counter, but that was of no real importance. What mattered was to get started in this class of competition.

The agreed price — 13,000 francs — gave him the car itself, a trailer and a few spare parts. Seppi paid in cash which left him exactly 11 francs in his pocket.

On the way back he was happy and proud. 'Remember, I'm not twenty-four yet and I've got my own racing car!' he told Michel, full of the joys of spring.

For its first outing on the 25th June the car was put in for the hill-climb at Rossens, a narrow, twisting track near Fribourg. Running broadside on more often than not, Seppi still managed to finish third with a time of 1 minute 07.6 seconds, only 4 seconds behind the winner — Michel Niquille on a Porsche.

Joseph and Michel then put in for some circuit races in Italy. Yvette went with them to Messina. It was a long run; if they went over 50 mph the trailer, pulled by an Opel Kapitan, began to sway dangerously. The expedition to Sicily was not particularly comfortable. They had to use what money they had first of all to buy petrol and spares for the Stanguellini; the food had to be paid for out of what was left. The nights were either spent driving or else sleeping on the back seat — or outside beside the car if it were fine and they weren't on the move. Next, Siffert entered for a hill-climb at Sierre-Montana in the Valais where Michel Piller and Gaby Guisolan spent most of the night repairing a half-shaft broken when he went off the road in practice. In the race, Siffert treated himself to the luxury of overtaking an Italian works driver but finished seventh in the overall classification.

From time to time the authorities of the town where the race meetings took place would lay on a reception. The Group Siffert would take advantage of this to make up for lost time on the eating side and also to stock up for the future. At Klagenfurt for example Joseph and Pierre Gross literally fell on the tomato canapes supplied by the Mayor on the evening of practice. Some delicacies don't lend themselves to speedy consumption; the little balls of caviar would often end up anywhere but their intended destination.

There were plenty of amusing incidents. Sometimes Seppi almost seemed to create them as a means of forgetting his problems. Coming back from a hill-climb at Urcy, which he had just won, the Group got to the Customs at 2 o'clock in the morning, hoping that the Customs people would be a bit dozy because the four passports that they had in hand were not really enough for the five people in the car: Seppi, his sister Adelaide who hadn't got any papers, Yvette, Fredy Haenni and his wife Monique. Joseph wound down the window and showed the officer the passports one by one, taking care not to leave them in his hands.

'Now let's look, here's mine. Good. This one is my mechanic's. Good. This one belongs to the one who is sleeping in the back. No it's not, it belongs to the other one who's sleeping.' In fact, nobody was asleep but all the occupants of the car were pinching themselves not to laugh out loud. Fed-up, the Customs man opened up all the baggage, going carefully through the contents of everything before letting the Opel through — without realizing that he had missed out a passport!

Around Fribourg Seppi was not well known. He raced mostly abroad and his qualities were quite overlooked. On the other hand, his supporters gave him every sort of encouragement though none of them at this time helped him financially.

His mother had gradually got used to the idea of his being a racing driver. When he set off, she would ask him not to drive too fast; her thoughts would be with him all the time. When he came back, and if he had not won, she would ask him: 'Couldn't you have gone a little bit faster?' Maria Siffert would always have for her son the same blend of reserve and encouragement, the same fears and hopes based on a complete trust in him.

Towards the end of the 1960 season, Seppi came to know Jean-Pierre Oberson, also aged twenty-four, a mechano-physicist and a former student of the Fribourg Technicum. One day Seppi asked him to stand in for Piller and come with him to a hill-climb at Gaisberg in Austria the next weekend. Jean-Pierre accepted, adding at the same time that motor mechanics were not at all his thing.

Seppi's activities in the motor trade increased considerably with the approach of winter: he wanted to accumulate some twenty thousand francs which would enable him to buy a new car to run during the next season. Siffert worked himself to the bone and at the beginning of January he made his trip to London in the Renault van, which is where this book started.

* * * * *

In the spring of 1961 Seppi suggested that Jean-Pierre might accompany his team right through the coming season. Jean-Pierre, whom Seppi had nicknamed Dumme, accepted the invitation all the more willingly as Michel would come to the majority of the meetings and would also inculcate him into the intricacies of the mechanics of a racing car. After the hill climb at Mont-sur-Rolle, Siffert was really going to try out the Lotus 18 on the Cesenatico circuit in Italy. After the practice, the drivers and journalists were discussing their views and trying to forecast what would happen in the race. Among then, Lucien Bonnet, the favourite, was voicing his fears of being beaten by the South African, John Love, who was driving a Formula Junior Cooper from Ken Tyrrell's stable. At this point, the well known Italian journalist, Franco Lini intervened: 'I saw a little Swiss this afternoon whom I don't know at all, but who seemed to me to be going very fast. If I were you, I should watch out for him.'

The writer from Milan was right. Siffert won the race and went to the top of the European Formula Junior Championship to the great joy of Jo Pasquier, a friend from Fribourg who had made the trip to Cesenatico just to see this Swiss who everyone was talking about in action. The following Sunday, on the Vallelunga circuit near Rome, Siffert confirmed his ability by coming in second behind the French driver, Henri Grandsire.

The atmosphere in the team and out in the world as well began to hot up. Siffert was now no longer the young beginner who went through all his corners sideways. The Lotus 18 allowed him to take an easier line which improved his efficiency and his results. But the preparation of his car was also a vital ingredient. A real doctor of machinery, Michel Piller went over the engine with a stethoscope after each race.

The trio went off together to Lake Garda where, leaving out Jim Clark and Trevor Taylor who had definitely moved on to Formula One, all the top drivers had turned out, including Colin Davis, David Piper, Henri Grandsire, Tony Maggs and John Love — the last two driving Coopers for Ken Tyrrell. After turning in some good times in practice, Seppi really tried in the race. In the final he went off the road, spinning it in the second last corner in front of the stands on the second lap; he was really pushing the favourites whom he overtook as his car spun. 'Do you realize,' he said afterwards, 'that I overtook all the front runners as I went off backwards!'

With an incredible bit of luck the Lotus came to a standstill less than a yard from a massive iron gate; Joseph slammed it into first gear and charged back into the race. He went through the field and found himself back in third place behind Love and Maggs. Then the two works Coopers had to pull into the pits with misfiring problems and had to have their plugs changed; Siffert moved into the lead and went on to win.

Among the spectators, not only his parents and friends had been impressed with his performance. Another one had been Jean-Claude Fontana, a photographer from Fribourg whom Seppi occasionally met in the Peacock Cafe there and whom he had started going to races. It was through him that after the race Signor Cotti invited the three Swiss to call the next day at his clothes shop and each fit themselves up with a complete outfit: navy blue blazer, shirt, tie, grey trousers, shoes — none of them had ever been so well dressed.

With two wins and a second place in three more races, the season looked very promising. But for the time being living conditions were not very much better. Seppi, Michel and Jean-Pierre slept on a mattress in the big Chevrolet station wagon. Michel and Jean-Pierre did turn and turn about sleeping on the front seat. Joseph had bought a tent but it was the racing car which enjoyed the benefit of that. The food supplies were bought by Jean-Pierre: meat, fruit, vegetables — the meals were not copious nor very varied but the food was wholesome. In addition to this, Mamma Siffert would give them honey and jam and coffee or Ovaltine, so their table was quite tempting, particularly as Dumme revealed himself as an excellent cook — so good indeed that David Piper, one of the British drivers, would eat with them as often as he was asked. In the end Bisule, who was rather better equipped, invited the Siffert Group to share his

61

caravan, but Jean-Pierre still carried on as chef for everyone.

Monaco was the last race Seppi would drive in with his Lotus 18. The factory was about to bring out a new model — the Lotus 20 — which Siffert would have to order if he was going to hold his position at the top of the European Championship. The engine on the 18 was finished. Pierre Gross and Jean-Claude Mulhauser obtained a new crankshaft ordered from the factory as quick as possible and got it over to the airport at Geneva, but it wasn't any good as it was badly scored. After admitting the defects in the crankshaft which had been sent to Geneva, Colin Chapman, the head of Lotus, agreed to lend them an engine for the race — one which had come out of Peter Arundell's car because it was vibrating badly. This meant driving with caution so that it did not blow up. As soon as it arrived the whole engine was stripped down. Michel then re-assembled it, noting all the marks and in particular the angles of the valves and cams; it was the first time he had worked on an engine set up by the works.

In the race Joseph naturally did not dare to force the pace and although it was entirely against his nature he played a waiting game and ended up with a fifth place. The Swiss journalist, Adrianno Cimarosti, still gave him a good write-up. But for the Group Siffert team, the real race didn't start until after the finish: Seppi wanted to off-load his Lotus 18 onto an Italian driver known as Geki who naturally didn't know that the Swiss had just been running his car on an engine lent him by the works. The engine which had to be returned to Colin Chapman was taken out in the garage and replaced by the original one. However, before making up his mind and paying for it, the purchaser wished to test the car once more himself on Monday at the Monza Autodrome. Seppi set off there, a little sceptical about a happy outcome for the affair. After two or three laps throughout which the engine bumped and banged alarmingly, Joseph declared that it was still cold and asked for his money without further delay, pretending that he had to go to a funeral that afternoon in Switzerland. The deal completed, Siffert received a suitcase full of notes which he counted and then drove off at full speed, without stopping, straight for the frontier and home. He was only just in time — as Geki, after doing a few more laps, burst the engine and informed the police . . .

Seppi set off in a Borgward van to take delivery of the new Lotus 20. The necessary funds not having been altogether collected in, Jo Pasquier a furrier in Fribourg had advanced him 3,000 francs which Seppi would have to return in the course of the following week. His first race was a handicap affair at Oulton Park and Siffert only finished ninth. Lucien Balsiger was happier about things: profiting from the absence of the English drivers at Chimay, he had quickly managed to settle accounts with Geki, his main rival, by winning the Grand Prix of Spain in Madrid and going a bit further by beating the lap record set up by the Marquis de Portago.

Siffert next drove in the 1000-kilometre race at the Nurburgring with Robert Jenny as co-driver sharing the wheel of a Ferrari Testa Rossa; it was his first real endurance test and gave him a chance to take in the formidable problems of a circuit over 14 miles long and with some 153 bends. The Siffert-Jenny partnership came third in the 2-litre class behind Bonnier and Moss.

On their return to Fribourg, Siffert and his mechanics got ready for an expedition lasting a month to drive in Italy and France. Michel took tremendous care to get the car right up to the mark in all respects, but the lack of a testing track made itself cruelly felt as no real checks could be carried out. Joseph had a word with the chief of the Canton Service des Automobiles, Monsieur Fernand Thorin, and asked if he could have permission to test his machine early one morning on the Pratzet Straight, which was about two miles long, between Fribourg and Bulle. Monsieur Thorin not only gave him permission but offered the services of two of his men from the Fribourg force with instructions to hold up traffic on the route. And so some of the local farmers were occasionally woken up at five in the morning by the unaccustomed roar of Seppi's red Lotus.

The preparations and organization didn't stop with the car. Siffert had to fit two extra fuel tanks to his Ford station wagon so that it could take 75 gallons of petrol — enough to get them from Fribourg to Sicily without filling up. The price of petrol was so much lower in Switzerland than in France or Italy that it was worth the trouble. As for the petrol pump men, told to fill her up, they just couldn't believe their eyes. After 25 gallons or so, they started to ease up on the flow, then they stopped altogether and got down under the car, thinking that it must have got a leak. Inside the station wagon Seppi and his mechanics laughed until they cried!

But Seppi wasn't always laughing — he could fly into the most appalling rages; having left his Lotus for several days in Robert Boschung's repair shop, the latter and Michel Piller decided between them to doll it up a little. When Seppi got back, the Lotus was tarted up like a chorus girl in bits of stuff and tissue paper.

'That's not a laughing matter, it's much too serious,' he shouted, livid with a rage which soon evaporated. He didn't bear malice or bottle things up. His frankness and spontaneity sometimes led him to come up with unpalatable truths. But then it was finished, he wouldn't speak of it again.

Right at the beginning of the summer, Seppi and Jean-Pierre set out together for Terramo in Italy. In the race there Love and Maggs quickly broke the engines of their Coopers and Siffert found himself leading the race. In the pits Dumme was acting as time-keeper. Robin of the French Edger Team and Ken Tyrrell watched the Swiss mechanic and were amazed at the way he kept the times.

A dream realised: Jo Siffert after winning
the British Grand Prix of 1968
Left to right: Chris Amon, Rob Walker,
Jo Siffert and Earl Mountbatten

Chris Amon gets a little impatient with
Jo Siffert who is leading the British Grand
Prix of 1968

A successful collaboration: Jo Siffert and Rob Walker

The driver and the sculptor: Jo Siffert and Jean Tinguely

'We haven't got a stopwatch,' Jean-Pierre told them, 'so each time he comes past I have to count in my head how many seconds' lead he has and then I signal it to him on the next lap.'

Seppi pulled out such a long lead that Dumme couldn't calculate it exactly. So he just contented himself with making a little sign as Seppi went by indicating that he had nothing to worry about as far as his pursuers were concerned and all he had to do was finish the race to win, which he did . . .

From there the two Swiss went on to Caserta near Naples. Going down Italy, they made sure of enough time to celebrate this new victory and enjoyed an evening of rejoicing. The next day the sun was beating down and Joseph and Jean-Pierre drove off feeling somewhat the worse for wear. Sitting beside Seppi who was driving, Dumme dozed, his face bathed in sweat.

'You don't find it hot?' Seppi enquired.

'Yes, I was just about to suggest stopping for a glass of beer.'

'We haven't got the time and we've got plenty of petrol,' said Seppi, who had a horror of stopping in the middle of a journey.

'I can feel a current of hot air on my feet — you don't thing we ought to stop and cool the engine down a bit?' suggested the mechanic, who could scarcely speak.

'No, the temperature gauge is not very far into the red.'

'It's no good, he won't stop,' thought Jean-Pierre who tried in vain to get to sleep. He was astonished at Seppi's extraordinary physical resistance; he even seemed to smile. Dumme couldn't understand it at all.

'You bastard,' he suddenly yelled at Seppi, who roared with laughter. 'You've had the heater turned on!'

In fact, Joseph had not only turned the heater on, but he had turned all the heat in the direction of his passenger, who was so thirsty that he would even have drunk holy water.

However, Siffert wasn't going to stop the car until they got to Caserta where he carried off a second place, just as he did at Aquila to the east of Rome the following Sunday.

From Italy Seppi and Dumme turned towards France to compete in the hill-climb at the Mont-Ventoux. The evening after practice Joseph asked Jean-Pierre to cook a dish of ravioli. By the time he had warmed up the tin, Seppi wasn't hungry any more. 'You can finish them,' he said to his mechanic after eating six or eight.

Jean-Pierre ate a few and then put the tin down.

'You're not going to throw that ravioli away?' said Siffert.

'It's you who wanted them — eat them yourself. I'm not hungry any more.'

'I'm not either and I can't force myself because I'm racing tomorrow. You'll have to finish them.'

So Jean-Pierre finished them and had a bad go of indigestion as a result: such was Seppi's extraordinary power of persuasion. Whether it was in business or in jest, his powers were almost magic; with a minimum of words, like a fakir he could hypnotise or persuade anyone to do what he wanted, whatever it might be.

The next day Seppi won the race and set up a new lap record, and then for the first time in four months invited Jean-Pierre to eat at a restaurant before going back to Switzerland; a return which passed unnoticed in spite of the dozen or so cups which he had won.

The next meeting of the Formula Junior circus was at Reims where Seppi particularly liked the very fast circuit, but where Bisule was much less happy in spite of his recent victory in Madrid. The two men talked things over between the practice sessions.

'You should be able to go a bit quicker,' Seppi said.

'I just don't know how: I think I am braking late at Thillois [which is the last bend before the stands] but I can feel that something is not quite right.'

66

'Are you taking your foot off at the top of the Annie Soibault corner?'

'I lift off a bit and then down again,'

'Try it with your foot right down on the floor; you'll see — it will swing less than if you back off. Try a lap behind me and follow my line exactly.'

Following Seppi, Bisule tried it out, but as he approached the crest his courage failed him: he lifted his foot just to gather up his courage and then pushed it down again.

Ahead of him, Joseph had gone through the corner perfectly and was twenty yards ahead of him.

'I took some more chances lifting my foot after that, but I didn't do very much better,' the Geneva driver recollected.

On race day on the start-line Lucien Balsiger felt very depressed. 'Wouldn't I be very much better sitting in the stands,' he asked himself, looking at the crowd. At the finish he told his friends that he was going to retire: 'It's all too fast,' he said, 'I can't keep up any more.'

Michel and Jean-Pierre set out alone for the Grand Prix of Messina; Joseph wanted an extra two days for business and would join them by air. The two mechanics soon found themselves short of money and provisions; all they had to eat the day before Seppi arrived was an ice-cream in the morning and another one in the afternoon.

In the race, Siffert had to retire when in the lead in the final and he flew straight home. The two mechanics drove all the way up Italy, put the car in order when they reached Fribourg, and then pushed on for the Nurburgring between Coblenz and Aix-la-Chappelle where Seppi put in a dashing drive in the Eifelrennen. According to the old tradition, he gained a 'Ring of Nurburg' — a memento given to every driver who mastered this circuit which is considered the most difficult in the world. After this, the ring — symbolising his bond with motor sport — never left Seppi's finger.

And then the team took the road back to Sicily again. The

thousands of miles that they covered towing that wretched trailer, which prevented them from making any real speed, were hard going: only the victories won or hoped for and an insane passion for motor sport helped to make them less arduous. Joseph had not yet fully realised his dream; certainly he was a racing driver, but his real objective was to join the international elite of Formula One and for the moment he had only got as far as Formula Junior.

Siffert was well aware that he couldn't rush things. His achievements so far had brought him honour and satisfaction, but the path to success had to be climbed step by step. And in any case his finances made it impossible for him to find any short cuts.

The turn-out at Enna-Pergusa was impressive: two works Ferraris for Giancarlo Baghetti and Lorenzo Bandini; John Love and Tony Maggs were driving Ken Tyrrell Coopers; Lotus had entered Colin Davis. Ecurie Edger were represented by Grandsire and Piper. At the end of practice Siffert was credited with third best time, which put him on the front row with the two Ferrari drivers who seemed unbeatable. However, realizing that Siffert, the independent, had the best opportunity to do something about them, Peter Warr, the Lotus team manager, supplied Seppi with some alternative gear ratios which were more suitable for the very fast circuit.

Armed with these, Seppi went out in front of the race keeping the Ferraris a few respectful lengths behind him and won the race. This didn't go down very well with the Ferrari team, nor with the second man in, Lorenzo Bandini. They lodged a protest claiming that Siffert's Lotus was below the minimum weight allowed of 420 kilos and that it had a 1300 cc engine instead of an 1100. The car was impounded and taken ten miles to the nearest public weighbridge: with battery, oil and water, it weighed exactly 420 kilos. Seppi knew this already because when he had taken delivery he had had to add some lead ballast to bring the car up to the

68

correct weight. The protesters wouldn't withdraw and insisted that the motor must be taken down and the cylinder capacity checked. Jean-Pierre and Seppi had to submit to this demand and they stripped the engine down themselves. Then the officials made the necessary calculations and confirmed that the total capacity was 1100 cc, and with that they went away, leaving Siffert and Oberson to reassemble the engine. And it had to be done properly because Seppi had no spare motor. At 10 o'clock that night, the race having finished five hours before, the two men had done the job and went to hear the official result announced without bothering to change.

Fortunately, Bandini was not there; the only common ground he had with Seppi was a mutual fury which would certainly have led to blows. Joseph received some cups, a cheque and went straight off.

It wasn't until the next day that the joys of victory erased the annoyances of all the investigation to which he had been subjected. They had to go straight off to Cadours, but not before he had ordered some replacement parts by telephone from England. In France, Seppi won again and set up a new lap record. He celebrated his third consecutive win with a fearful night out in the company of Jo Schlesser who was recovering from an accident at Le Mans.

On the way back to Fribourg he found time to put through a few deals and then they went to Montlhery where he wanted to take part in two events running — the Coupe du Salon and the Coupe de Paris. Michel Piller didn't go with him but Jean-Pierre did, and several other friends as well: among them Jean-Claude Fontana, Michel Bulliard, Fredy Haenni, Georges Blanc, Kuno Glauser and Pierre Gross. Third in the first race, Siffert who slept in the pits underneath the racetrack was favourite for the second, which would be run on the following Sunday. So much so that the Race Director, wanting to keep up interest in the race, asked him not to start off too fast. Joseph agreed, and stayed with the leading group in which there were no major drivers, and then went out ahead to an inevitable victory.

One problem presented itself after he had crossed the finishing line — Seppi hadn't got a clean white shirt for the prizegiving. He had only got the one he had been wearing for the last three days. A solution was soon thought up; all he needed was a piece of chalk! No sooner said than done: Monique Haenni was given the delicate task of whitening the collar and cuffs of Seppi's shirt. Nobody noticed in the hot smoky atmosphere of the prizegiving and the personal allure of the winner isn't the most important consideration at the ceremony. And it didn't prevent Group Siffert from laying down the law at the party which followed. The champagne vanished as quickly as it appeared and the other guests, like Siffert's adversaries, soon ceased to exist.

It was a great party. In a way it marked the end of the 1961 season. Joseph Siffert was the European Formula Junior Champion — an official title awarded by an Italian newspaper which sponsored most of the events — and winner of the International Trophy. The title didn't bring him in any contracts nor did it get him signed up with any of the works teams. Peter Warr, the Lotus team manager, was convinced of Seppi's courage — they had become good friends — and there was even a question of signing him up, but Colin Chapman was against it from motives of patriotism. This was fair enough: as long as Britain was producing the best drivers, the Lotus factory could hardly take on a foreigner. So Siffert started the next year on his own.

In November accompanied by Jean-Pierre, Michel Bulliard and Norbert Riedo he went to London where, after 'officially' celebrating the season and his title as European Champion, he handed over to Lotus the deposit on a Model 22, a Formula One car, for which he placed an order.

On return to Fribourg, he retired to his winter quarters and concentrated exclusively on his secondhand car business.

70

Twice a day Jean-Pierre made the trip from Fribourg to Geneva to bring back the cars, usually crashed ones, which Seppi had bought. Thoroughly renovated, the bumps ironed out, the bangers always fairly gleamed; the dealers who came to Seppi from German-speaking Switzerland, bought them up five at a time after interminable arguments over the price. On this Seppi would not give way — he was a real shark. He would haggle for hours over fifty francs and he wouldn't clinch the deal if he didn't get his way. *'Tr'a nit'* — I cannot, in the German-Swiss dialect — he would repeat endlessly to clients who tried to get him to lower the price. A racing car was so expensive . . . and Seppi thought only of that.

* * * * *

Seppi's sporting and business activities brought him into contact with many people and he came to be friends with many of them. Young people of his own age found his personality attractive and he had many friends. In this way he became an acquaintance of Guy von der Weid, a horseman who had bought a car from him and liked him. Another was Paul Blancpain, then aged eighteen, who met him one day in the Rex tearooms, a great rendezvous for the young Fribourgeois. Coming from a large family of brewers, Paul was working for a Fribourg architect specializing in building churches. The boot of his car was stuffed with plans and models and he would visit suburban vicarages, presbyteries and bishops' palaces in France where every now and again he would find a church which pleased him — not only from the functional and economic point of view, but also on the level of sacred art.

The female kind had also begun to interest themselves in the racing driver and Seppi quickly became friends with a girl called Sabine, a model who soon made him forget Yvette.

Joseph was not insensitive to the affections of his fans who would travel hundreds of miles at night to give him a hand. However, in spite of the help he got and the amount of work done, Siffert still did not have enough money for the coming season. Seppi decided to launch a fund which was entitled 'A Formula One Car for Siffert'. Thanks to the efforts of his friends, and in particular to the zeal of Jo Pasquier, over 6000 tickets were sold especially in cafes all over Switzerland. Although the operation made a large profit of which Seppi had the benefit, it only served to postpone his financial problems. In the end Joseph's supporters formed a motor racing group called the Ecurie Fribourgeois.

At the same time an Ecurie Nationale Suisse — with the object of encouraging young talent — had been formed in Geneva by Georges Filipinetti, who, after some pressure from the ACS, soon re-named it the Scuderia Filipinetti. Having noticed Siffert's several successes, the journalist Henri-Francois Berchet advised him to secure the services in Formula One of the talented Fribourgeois driver. Thinking that he had found the answer to his cash problem, the latter accepted the offer which was signed and sealed on the 13th March 1962 — the first agreement with the Geneva stable running for three years. On the 23rd June of the same year, he signed a second agreement which bound him to abide by its clauses until the end of 1965!

The Filipinetti team had enough money, of course, but Joseph had lost his liberty. He felt himself pinned down.

Siffert began the season in Formula Junior on his own account. And he started off well by repeating his victory of the year before at Cesenatico, this time with the Lotus 22. Then it was the Grand Prix of the Lake of Garda near Brescia where everyone thought he would also carry off a double after his win there in 1961. Siffert duly got himself onto the front row on the Saturday. His friend, Georges Blanc, who had a business selling lorries and Cadillac cars near Vevey, Fontana the photographer, Pasquier the furrier and Balsiger who was now a Siffert-supporter, were all confident: victory could not escape Seppi. Then the organizers raised a few problems — they claimed that his gearbox was not homologated. In fact, the Lotus 22 was fitted with a new Hewland box which was a standard unit on the latest Volkswagen of which the first cars were just coming onto the market. Seppi, who had seen one in Brescia, chased after it and managed to catch it. Without too much trouble, he persuaded the owner, a German tourist, to show it to the officials, the organizers couldn't say any more and they allowed Seppi to start in the race.

In the final, Siffert was on the front row as expected, with the winner of the second heat. Beside the track Georges Blanc remarked that the radiator seemed to be spilling a few drops of water but Siffert wasn't too worried about it and shot off with a roar. The circuit is a long one. The first time round Joseph was so far ahead of everyone else that some people thought that there must have been a pile-up involving the main pack. In fact, the runners-up completed their lap fifteen seconds behind the Swiss. The issue seemed settled already. On the second lap, Seppi had lost most of his lead and was making signs to the pits. On the third lap, he pulled in; the temperature gauge was reading so high that he didn't dare go on. Piller and Oberson didn't take long finding out what was the matter; the radiator was empty. Then they discovered a split made with a knife just at the top of the connecting water hose pipe. Someone had made a small nick in the pipe which had enlarged under pressure and through which the water had escaped. Furious, Joseph was almost in tears, tears of rage.

The Sunday following the first April was a great day: for the first time Siffert was starting in a Formula One race, the Brussels Grand Prix. The Lotus 24 had not yet been delivered by the factory so Colin Chapman had lent him a 1500 engine, dry sump, with two Weber carburettors, which after some detail alteration was installed in the Formula Junior car.

In the race Seppi, who took advantage of the rain to exploit his exceptional driving skill, tried to hang on to Stirling Moss. But suddenly in a bend just after an underpass, the great Stirling, then driving for Rob Walker, had to take to the escape road. As it happened, Seppi came unstuck as well, thus avoiding a collision, and the two of them waltzed off together like two circus ponies. Then Moss and Siffert recovered their line and accelerated away again as if nothing had happened. Joseph finished the race in sixth place in front of the Porsches of Beaufort and Schiller; the victory went to Willy Mairesse.

Colin Chapman was worried about the engine which he had lent to Seppi. 'How many revs did you use?' he asked Seppi, convinced that his instruction had not been followed.

'Just what you told me,' Seppi replied.

Chapman made a face, signifying that he didn't believe a word of it.

'You see that?' Seppi said to Bisule. 'That ape doesn't believe anything I tell him!'

When they got back to Fribourg Joseph, Michel and Jean-Pierre took the chance to re-instal the Formula Junior engine into the Lotus and then they set out for Austria where he was going to take part in the Grand Prix of Vienna. On their way, in the middle of the night, as it was pouring with rain, a Fiat Topolino overtook them.

'Bad luck,' said Seppi, 'that poor chap is certainly going to run a big end.'

He had hardly finished speaking when the right twin rear wheels of the old Borgward they used to transport the Lotus came right off — the bolts had suddenly snapped. There wasn't a garage anywhere near. The three men tried to repair it with what they had on board but it took so long that the Group finally arrived after last practice was over. As a special favour, because of his European Championship title, the organizers allowed Siffert onto the track early on the

74

morning of the race and they allowed him to start in it, although from the back row. Joseph wasn't too much hampered by this. He won his heat and the final, and shattered the lap record for good measure. The following Sunday the 24th April, Seppi travelled empty to Pau: the Lotus team would bring out the Lotus 24, with a Climax 4-cylinder engine, ordered by the Scuderia Filipinetti. Joseph, Michel, Jean-Pierre, Bisule — they were all anxious to see the new machine which would enable the Swiss driver to make his first real entry into the world of Formula One.

But disillusion soon dashed his hopes: after they had helped to unload the two Lotus of Jim Clark and Trevor Taylor, the Group Siffert found at the bottom of the lorry a completely bare Formula One chassis; it had wheels but no engine, no gearbox, no tank, no coachwork!

'You can take it or leave it,' said Chapman to Baudoin, the Filipinetti manager — who had been told not to pay for the car if it wasn't complete.

'But yes — we have got a day and a half to put it together,' urged Seppi who was ready to do anything rather than see the car go back to England. So the car was unloaded in sections.

The assembly was not quite as easy as they had anticipated. Michel, Jean-Pierre and Bisule now realized that the sump had to be removed because the engine, designed to be mounted flat, should according to the specification be fitted at an angle.

'At this time the finish of the racing cars wasn't all that good,' Peter Warr said later; it was also customary in England to deliver racing cars in broken-down sections for reasons of tax, or in the case of abroad, customs duty.

After working all day and night to assemble the jigsaw puzzle, the mechanics could at last get on with the checking and testing, which revealed among other things that the Colotti gearbox which had pressure lubrication was broken.

By chance, Alf Francis had one to spare.

All these problems considerably delayed the preparation of the Lotus which wasn't ready for the first practice. So Joseph just had to wait until second practice before hitting the track at the wheel of a Lotus 24, absolutely untested; running in, roadholding, everything still had to be done, for this new and inexperienced contender in Formula One.

Siffert still managed to qualify. In the race, Taylor went out on the 18th lap followed by Clark six laps later. The two works Lotus were parked behind the pits. Chapman left his pit and came over to help with Siffert's team for the rest of the race. Siffert finished sixth, although the oil pressure was dropping dangerously low. The race was won by Maurice Trintignant upholding the colours of Rob Walker whose other driver, Stirling Moss, had met with a serious accident at Goodwood on the same day — the accident which put him out of motor racing for good.

Joseph Siffert next ran in the last Formula Junior of his career at Berlin on the Avus circuit. Jean-Pierre and David Raymond, a young car salesman whom Seppi had taken on, went with him so that Michel could stay in Fribourg to finish working up the Formula One car that had been handed over to them in Pau.

With best time in practice, Seppi saw his chances of winning improve still more when Peter Warr gave him a higher fifth gear ratio. By way of thanking him, Joseph gave Peter an identical helmet to the one he liked to wear himself with the white cross on a red ground. In the race, he carried off the victory which he had counted on with brio, and he had the signal privilege of doing his lap of honour escorted by Mayor Willy Brandt and the German Chancellor Ludwig Erhard.

The distribution of prizes did not take place until the Monday morning so the victory had to be celebrated with decorum — in the Smocky Bar, where Jean-Pierre drank 140

Deutschmarks' worth of beer and cognac. Some other Swiss who had also been competing but in a different category and who had also won, joined the Fribourgeois. It was a good party.

Back in Switzerland, the group set off again on the Wednesday afternoon for Naples to run in a Formula One epreuve there, but they hadn't allowed enough time and the car didn't reach the circuit until after the end of practice. Siffert tried to argue his way in, but for once he failed to persuade the organizers to let him start. The mechanics were less disappointed than Seppi — they wanted to have a good sleep before packing back to Switzerland.

The Grand Prix of Monaco was the first race counting for the Drivers' World Championship in which Joseph had been entered. Fredy Haenni who, at the last moment, had replaced Michel Piller — he was ill — and Jean-Pierre Oberson went with him. Siffert's Lotus which would have to qualify, was the only single-seater with a four-cylinder engine; all the other cars had gone over to the new V8 engines.

Seppi did the impossible to qualify and found a cunning ruse: at this time the startline and the timekeepers' station were situated behind the pits just before the Gasworks Hairpin. To clock in a good time Joseph braked before the line, began the new lap under acceleration right over to the left to take the best line through the Gasworks Corner, then completed the lap without lifting his foot until he had crossed the line — if he arrived at the Gasworks Corner all crossed up for his next lap it didn't matter. The drill was valuable: the best time out of two is the one that counts. Seppi just managed to qualify: he made eighteenth place — the last. Innes Ireland who made exactly the same time but after Seppi saw himself pipped.

Georges Filipinetti was so pleased that he gave a party for his protegé and his mechanics. However, late that night, when the numbers had already been painted on the starting grid, officials arrived at the Hotel Suisse; the Fribourgeois were woken up and Seppi was told that there had been a mistake and Ireland's time had in fact been turned in earlier and so he would start. The next morning Siffert went to the time-keepers' office, he was quite certain that the original times had been correct, but he couldn't do anything to change their minds. Joseph was terribly upset. As it was he took part in his first World Championship event on the 17th June in the Grand Prix of Belgium at Spa in which he finished in tenth place.

At Reims where there was a sort of dress rehearsal for the French Grand Prix which would be held the following Sunday at Rouen, a violent quarrel broke out between Joseph and Michel — who decided to quit; he went back to Fribourg the Saturday before the race where he would open a small agency for Abarth and specialize in the preparation of competition cars.

The new BRM V8 engines arrived for Rouen and Siffert wanted to try it immediately, although Filipinetti wanted to run once more on the 4-cylinder Climax. On the sixth lap he had to retire with clutch trouble. Paul Blancpain who had come for the race began to work in with Group Siffert giving them an occasional helping hand.

On the administrative side not everything was left to the Ecurie Filipinetti; the photographer and decorator, Jean-Claude Fontana, had designed a letterhead and Michel Bulliard, a friend of Seppi, acted a little as manager. The racing car was always kept at Fribourg. Michel Piller whom Joseph had not succeeded in persuading to return was replaced by Heini Mader, a first class mechanic who till then had been responsible for the Schiller Porsche in Geneva.

Relations between Siffert and Filipinetti didn't improve at the Grand Prix de la Solitude near Stuttgart and Siffert became more and more anxious to recover his liberty even if it would bring endless problems in its train. But Seppi was also well aware that his contract ran for five years and that Filipinetti wouldn't let him go without an indemnity.

In the German Grand Prix Siffert was punished. After the trouble over the retirement at Solitude, Filipinetti decided not to give him the BRM V8 engine but to let him run with the old Climax 4-cylinder. Joseph tried to be patient and agreed: he finished the race in twelfth position.

In mid-August Siffert tried again with the 8-cylinder and came in fourth at Enna, and then in Formula Junior he came first in two hill climbs at Ollon-Villars and Chamrousse. At Monza which would be the last race of the 1962 season he only did a few laps in practice — there was some defect in the gearbox. On the telephone from Geneva Georges Filipinetti ordered him to repair the car and to come back to Switzerland.

In the end, so as to keep his hand firmly on the organization, Filipinetti wanted to transfer the car and the mechanics from Geneva. Siffert refused categorically — on the contrary seeking to detach himself more and more from his patron. The workshop at the Wheatsheaf had become too small and Paul Blancpain started to look for something bigger which would also leave room to house and repair the secondhand cars. Some six or seven miles from Fribourg, the old Mouret Forge was to let — but the owner was still rather hoping to see horses around the place.

'Times change and we will be working on horsepower!' Paul told him, and gave him three months' rent.

Group Siffert installed themselves in their new quarters. The winter would be long and hard. Siffert worked harder than ever because he realized now that he couldn't remain much longer in the Filipinetti organization.

CHAPTER FOUR

During the lull between the 1962 and 1963 seasons Joseph pulled off a number of profitable deals. With a bulging briefcase he went to Geneva to see Georges Filipinetti and asked for his independence, or at least for much more liberty. The discussion was prolonged and complex. Finally Siffert bought back for a large sum the Lotus BRM which he had run for part of the last season. The agreement between the patron and his driver laid down that Seppi should still run under Ecurie Filipinetti colours, but with his own machine and his own organization. Paul Blancpain would organize the entries and other business matters. The two mechanics, Heini Mader and Jean-Pierre Oberson, would be entirely at Seppi's disposal. Starting money and prizes would still be shared with Ecurie Filipinetti.

Siffert decided to send the car back to the BRM works at Bourne to be prepared for the season which would open in March. The expedition was taken seriously: wearing their best suits, Paul, Heini and Jean-Pierre arrived at the factory to meet Wilkie Wilkinson who had managed the old Ecurie Ecosse. Conversation was a bit awkward as the three Swiss couldn't speak a word of English; and the manager did not know any language but his own. The engine was handed over to the workshop where it was worked on through the following day with Mader taking a hand. Mader's formidable mechanical skills made a deep impression on the technicians from the works. Making good use of the facilities of the factory, Jean-Pierre produced a new exhaust system and revised the back-end layout of the Lotus BRM.

The car was therefore in first class nick for its first race at Snetterton on the 22nd March. Seppi was delighted in spite of the paltry starting money he was given: 'She has never gone so well,' he said after a few practice laps. Then it started to rain, making the track slippery. Suddenly Siffert was missing. The Lotus had gone off the track on the fastest section, running through a pool of water at over 150 mph, and had finished up a hundred yards off in a field up to its exhaust in mud. By sheer bad luck, the chassis had hit a boundary stone in the field and couldn't be repaired for the race the next day. Joseph himself had escaped with a good fright. 'In the space of one or two seconds I had seen the whole of my life parading before me like a sort of memorial,' he told me afterwards.

The season had begun badly. On return to Fribourg where the chassis was straightened out, Seppi was very depressed. Exhausted by the work he had put in during the winter, his only reward had been to run off the road! On top of that, things were not going at all well with Sabine. Joseph was fed-up with everything. Not knowing what to do about all his troubles, he went round to his friends one Sunday night who tried to calm him down. 'What am I going to do? How can I get enough money for the next race?' he asked them.

'Don't worry, everything has been taken care of,' replied Paul and Jo Pasquier, and they took him practically by force to the station. 'Here is your ticket for Setes. The next race is at Pau. We will meet you on Thursday midday outside the last hotel going out of Setes in the direction of Pau.'

At the appointed time on Thursday a metallic grey Chevrolet Impala, exchanged by Paul for the Ford in Geneva, stopped on the outskirts of Setes to pick up Joseph Siffert, himself again now, calm, cheerful and cunning.

Before the start of the race the Group realized with amazement that their friend, Guy von der Weid, was sitting in the official car which had to close the circuit. In fact Guy had relations in Pau and he managed to get Siffert's starting money doubled. Siffert, however, had to retire halfway through the race, the brakes having failed just before going through the chicane when he was driving in company with the Dutch driver, Carel de Beaufort. The courage and tenacity he had shown during the race had not however escaped the notice of the experts. Toto Roche, the Race Director, paid tribute to Jim Clark the winner, and to Seppi. Joseph very much appreciated this. He hadn't any time to waste, however: next Sunday he was running in the Grand Prix of Imola near Bologna where he got a very good second place behind the unbeatable Jim Clark and in front of Bob Anderson. The achievement went down well. His father, Alois Siffert, could hardly hide his emotion. Clark himself congratulated his brilliant second with an encouraging: 'At Syracuse you will win!'

Joseph, Paul, Heini and Pierre set off once again: Bologna, Pescara, Bari, Taranto. They drove without stopping for a day and a half, taking turns to sleep and arrived in Sicily on time, where the prediction of Clark, who was not racing, came true: Joseph Siffert won his first Formula One victory the 25th April 1963 in Syracuse.

His pleasure was immense. Too great perhaps for it to show. Real pleasure is inside. The four Swiss didn't miss out on a celebration of their victory but they had a burning desire to get home. The Chevrolet Impala set off up the leg of Italy once again the next day, towing behind it the Lotus-Ford which for once Seppi did not mind seeing all dirty; it was the dust and grime of his first big win. For the first time also Jean-Pierre did not complain of thirst nor insist that they stop. The tension mounted with the miles; they all felt themselves heroes as they drove through the Gruyere on

82

the last lap before home and the six or seven cups they had loaded in with them burned their fingers.

At Fribourg the impact of the victory had been important enough and widely reported in the Press, but it was yesterday . . . The friends alone were still under the sway of emotion; for the public, it was really all over, but they could not remain cold and once again began to take up an interest.

The next Formula One race took place a fortnight later at Rome and did not count for the World Championship. Seppi would very much have liked to enter, particularly as the field would be more or less the same as at Syracuse. But Filipinetti was reluctant to give his agreement because the race at Rome would only precede by one week the Monaco Grand Prix at which the Écurie Filipinetti would absolutely have to be represented. Joseph himself would have preferred to win the race in Rome rather than run at Monaco. After a long telephone conversation with Georges Filipinetti, Paul woke Jean-Pierre and Heini and the outfit set out for Italy as soon as possible. It was 11 o'clock at night.

But on his arrival in Rome Seppi found himself barred from the track. The Écurie Filipinetti would not either officially enter the car or authorise Siffert to race on his own account.

It was too much. Seppi was beside himself; he wanted to terminate all co-operation with Filipinetti who, for his part, suggested that Seppi should run at Monaco and discuss things afterwards: 'I would rather go and listen to the cowbells on the Berra [a mountain near Fribourg] than drive for you at Monaco!' Joseph shouted by way of reply. Then he softened a little and said he would run but on the express condition that things would be sorted out the week after.

Filipinetti acceded to this, then said that the car must be brought to the Principality in the big truck that the Écurie Filipinetti had just bought. Deadlock again. Then more arguing. A new agreement: the Lotus would travel on the trailer as usual; the truck would drive down empty so as to ensure transport from the circuit to the garage between practice and the race.

As in the year before, the Siffert Group lodged in the Hotel Suisse. At 7 o'clock on the morning of the first practice, an official telephoned Seppi: 'Bad news, Monsieur Siffert. The Ecurie Filipinetti truck has gone off the road on a bend and crashed into a ravine. The driver is all right but I am afraid that your car has probably been badly damaged.'

'Don't worry at all — it will be ready for practice,' replied Joseph, putting the receiver back with a great bellow of laughter.

For the race Siffert received one instruction which did not agree well with his temperament: on no account was he to overtake Jo Bonnier. Before they had gone past the Casino for the first time, the Swiss could see the Swede in his rear view mirror. But the engine soon broke and on the fourth lap Seppi retired.

The next day he contacted Monsieur Philippe von der Weid, a lawyer and President of the ACS Fribourg, and the liquidation meeting took place on Tuesday in Geneva. There 'having recorded that they have different interpretations on the subjects of the application and of the execution of the contract of the 23rd June 1962 and also on the verbal agreements which followed, the parties agree definitely to bring to an end their lawful joint enterprise'. By a deed signed on the 28th May 1963 Siffert further agreed, so as to be completely free, to pay two sums of 10,000 francs. When both amounts fell due, Guy would advance any amount outstanding in spite of the banker's astonishment at his lending to a racing driver. 'He's a friend,' Guy told him, 'and then one has to be mad sometimes in one's life!'

Not very well informed, the Press the next day published a rather distorted account of what had happened. Seppi decided to call a press conference which he held on the same evening at the Mouret Forge workshop. Aged seventeen, just down from College, and the Fribourg sporting correspondent of the *Tribune de Geneve* for the last eight months, I met Siffert officially for the first time there. A contact was established immediately. I was amazed by so much courage and determination, a little bit dazzled by the roar of his racing car — the first I had seen close up — and I felt drawn into this new world where the personality of Joseph fascinated me. From that day Siffert had one more friend, another 'unconditional', who would render him a few small services in exchange for the school of life which the racing driver would open up for the young student.

Rico Steinemann, who had just launched a specialist magazine *'Powerslide'*, was also influenced by Joseph's tremendous willpower which fired the Siffert supporters; he also promised any help he could provide.

Joseph competed in his first Formula One race as an independent at Spa in the Belgian Grand Prix. On the seventeenth lap in the mix-up before the difficult La Source corner the Lotus suddenly spun off sideways and hit the bank with its back end. Seppi was parted from his car by the sudden impact and thrown right out; after turning a somersault he picked himself up unhurt. Fortunately the car was not badly damaged, but even so it was taken back to England for repairs. In Holland, at Zandvoort, Joseph and Jim Hall fought a merciless duel for sixth place which was finally won by the American driver; Seppi therefore just missed a first Championship point.

This first point in the Championship Siffert won a week later at Reims where a strong Fribourg contingent attended the French Grand Prix. As at Pau, Toto Roche was warm in his praise for the Swiss for whom he predicted a brilliant future when the results were announced. There was great rejoicing: for the independent Siffert who would in the future figure in the Drivers' World Championship figures; for his mother; for the mechanics who could now see more clearly the aim and purpose for which all their sacrifices were made; for his chums, for the Siffert Group who had a major celebration over the result.

Joseph had to retire in the British Grand Prix, but he passed yet another stage in his career: at the meeting of the GPDA — the Grand Prix Drivers' Association — which followed the first practice, Jo Bonnier and Jim Clark proposed a new member in the person of Joseph Siffert.

The Siffert Racing Team no longer slept under canvas or in the car; now they put up at hotels, although admittedly the cheaper ones. So as not to appear too shabby a figure in the Formula One Scene, Joseph felt that he must improve his standing a little, but always with an eye to economy.

Always dreaded, the unexpected happened the following Sunday at Stuttgart for the Grand Prix de la Solitude. As well as the team, several friends were there, among them Guy and Jo Pasquier who amused themselves by abstracting the pass stuck to the Race Director's windscreen, and found themselves being escorted as far as the circuit by two 'motards!' So far, so good — then in mid-race, Seppi had to retire: the Lotus had suddenly begun to disintegrate. The chassis was broken, the crankshaft as well, and on top of that the gearbox had seized.

Next Sunday Siffert was entered for the German Grand Prix. He had to move fast. Thinking rapidly, he worked out a plan of battle: the first thing was to take out the engine and gearbox. Guy would drive the BRM engine and Heini to Kloten and would go from there straight to the English factory; Paul would take the gearbox to Colotti where it could be repaired; Jean-Pierre would go straight to the Nurburgring and install himself in the paddock where he could repair the chassis; and Seppi himself would go back to Fribourg to get through as much business as he could. The team would rendezvous on Thursday night at the Nurburgring with all the repairs carried out and the car ready for practice.

The operation was a complete success. The exploit was so remarkable that it was written up by Rob Walker in the next edition of *Autosport*. Mader not only brought back the restored engine, but also a new BRM fuel-injection V8 which Seppi had ordered some time before. But the whole affair had been expensive — the crankshaft cost 9,000 francs and the repairs to the gearbox another 3,000, without taking into account any of the travelling costs.

Practice on Thursday had hardly started when the crankshaft of the new engine which Seppi was running in broke. The old engine was installed. In the race, all was going well and Joseph was lying fourth when, two laps from the finish, that crankshaft went as well. Classified ninth, Siffert was desperate: his financial resources had been stretched beyond the limit — the three crankshafts had cost him 27,000 francs. For the first time Joseph thought that he would really have to stop racing — he had no more means, no help.

Seppi decided however to have one last try — the Mediterranean Grand Prix at Enna a fortnight later — where he got a fifth place. For the time being the day was saved; morale which was essential had been restored; as for the money, they would just have to work even harder.

The next event was the hill-climb at Ollon-Villars, the Swiss Mountain Grand Prix. On the advice of Jo Pasquier I telephoned 'Monsieur Siffert' whom I had not seen since the press conference at the Mouret Forge; after congratulating him on his fifth place I asked if I could accompany him to Ollon.

'But of course — I shall be leaving the works at 4 o'clock on Wednesday,' he replied.

To ride with a Formula One driver was an event of some importance, and made a great impression on me. There was just time to make his acquaintance and then we were at

Ollon. Second in the race behind Jo Bonnier on a Ferguson four-wheel-drive car, Joseph took charge of me the next day and the return journey took in numerous stops at breakers' yards and second-hand car dealers in the Suisse Romande.

The Austrian and Italian Grands Prix were not very successful but thanks to the starting money, which was improving, the financial situation remained healthy so that a trip to America could not be ruled out, arrangements could be made.

Before that, Joseph still had to take part in the Gold Cup race at Oulton Park and, more important, he was going to marry Sabine before his departure. The marriage wouldn't be official until it was ratified by the Civil Registrar and the religious ceremony took place the evening before the date announced!

* * * * *

Accepted now by all the Formula One drivers, Jo Siffert would have liked to be properly recognised in the world of motor racing and in particular by the Grand Prix organizers. To do this he thought that the serious intentions of the Siffert Racing Team should be demonstrated by their taking part in all the races counting for the World Championship. From the end of August Joseph set about making all the necessary contacts so that he could enter for the next two Grands Prix of the season — the United States and Mexican Grands Prix.

Things did not go smoothly: the organizers did not reply to the letters sent by Paul. Finally, with Jo Bonnier's help, a deal was fixed up by telephone — the calls being made for reasons of economy from the house of Paul's parents in Nonan! The agreement was not particularly advantageous; Seppi would not receive any starting money but he would not have to pay for the transport of his car. It was a bit stingy. However, it was a start and now he would have to try and pick up a few windfalls for the expedition not to end in catastrophe.

Paul was not indispensable so Joseph decided to take only the two mechanics, Heini and Jean-Pierre. However, the team manager said that he would pay for his own expenses by selling his car — a Fiat 600 — to which Seppi agreed.

Anxious to make some new contacts for *Powerslide*, Rico Steinemann promised to lend a hand at the United States Grand Prix but, like Siffert, he was running economically. The two men combined forces: in exchange for a big reduction on the price of their tickets, Rico gave BOAC several pages of free publicity in his magazine. In addition, Seppi would pose for a photograph on the gangway just before leaving.

With the idea of making the best possible impression, Siffert and Blancpain decided to learn English. An American student at Fribourg University agreed to give them some lessons. For the first session which was really to make contact Seppi was only a quarter of an hour late.

The second lesson was almost over by the time Joseph arrived, held up by the sale of a car. However, he suggested an extension of half an hour in which they could go over again the bits he had missed. The American student then suggested that they should study the conjugation of the verbs.

'What do you mean by conjugate?' enquired Siffert, who remembered absolutely nothing from his schooldays except that he had been bored stiff!

So as to be sure of starting the third lesson on time, Seppi decided to fetch the student-professor himself. But on the appointed day he forgot all about the rendezvous and went to Geneva to look for a car. After that, he decided not to pursue his English studies, even in private!

Having learned both French and German simultaneously,

Siffert could express himself clearly in both languages — but no more than that. His vocabulary was purely utilitarian. His writing was also affected by this bi-lingualism and Joseph never acquired the secret of good spelling or style.

If this gap had something to do with his shyness when confronted by people he did not know, Joseph didn't care: he preferred to observe, registering with his personality what others lost in well-turned phrases. Without being a great talker, he could always make himself understood with a glance or by the expression of his face.

The day before he left for America, Joseph went to the bank: 'I would like to change 500 Swiss francs into dollars,' he told the cashier.

'You're going to America for the first time and only staying for the race?' asked the cashier, who knew him quite well.

'No, I'm staying for a month with my two mechanics and my manager.'

The cashier couldn't get over it. He knew that Siffert lived as simply as possible, but even so he tried to get him to take a little bit more money. In the end Seppi gave way and bought 500 dollars, although not without promising that he would bring them all back on his return.

Siffert, Blancpain and Steinemann met up in London with Mader and Oberson — they had stayed in England after Oulton Park — and the five Swiss flew off together to discover America. As soon as they arrived Paul telephoned his cousin, Jean-Daniel de Schaller who lived in New York and asked him to put them up for the night. The five men installed themselves in a studio with only one bed where they spent two nights — not perhaps very comfortably but at least free of charge.

For the first time, Siffert found himself at the wheel of a brand new car: Ford had put a car at the disposal of every driver in the US Grand Prix to get them to the Watkins Glen circuit about 3Q0 miles from New York, where Joseph had hired a cabin for three dollars a day with three beds and a shower; two of them took turns to sleep in the Ford. The menus were simple: cornflakes, hamburgers and milk or one cigar — the result was the same — it took the edge of their hunger.

One evening Joseph was invited to a reception and his bodyguard went as well: John-Pierre, Heini, Paul and Rico. Stupefied, eyes goggling, they contemplated the riches of the buffet. Seppi retained his presence of mind: 'It's my party,' he told them. 'Let's get stuffing!'

Group Siffert fell on the dishes and did themselves proud. The five men literally gobbled everything which came to hand. Then, their stomachs full, they stocked up with reserves; one after the other, they wrapped in paper napkins or tucked into their pockets legs of chicken, cakes, ham, bottles of coke, and anything else which they could load into the car.

On the day before the race, the 4th October, Joseph Siffert took part in his first meeting of the GPDA of which he had now become an accepted member.

Things did not turn out for the best in practice: Seppi got ninth best time but the chassis of the Lotus broke and Jean-Pierre had to spend the whole night before the race welding it up. In the race, the engine seemed to hold up but a gear wheel broke in the gearbox soon after the halfway mark, and that was that.

The next day thanks to the intervention of Bonnier and after numerous discussions with Steinemann, Seppi was given a 300-dollar bonus by the organizers and the team set off back to New York that night. Sitting in the back, Joseph remained silent; he was working out how to avoid paying the 6 dollars toll at the end of the motorway. Suddenly he exclaimed: 'That's it, I've got it. We'll go past the last exit before the end of the motorway and then, where there's a sliding barrier between the track, we'll make a turn and go back to the exit as if we had come from New York. When we have got there we'll say that we have lost our ticket and it can't cost us more than one dollar.'

The occupants of the car thought this a good idea. After they had passed the last exit but one, the Ford stopped, all lights out. Paul got out and acted as scout on the strip of grass between the twin tracks. At a propitious moment the car crossed the grass dividing line, Paul climbed back in and they set off on the New York to Buffalo route. At the first exit the driver pretended to search for the ticket which he could not find. In the back Seppi was thumping Jean-Pierre, suddenly taken with a fit of giggles. The motorway man wasn't joking. He made them all get out and start searching. The operation had turned sour: they had to hide the tickets for good.

Siffert didn't realize his mistake until he had to pay the 12 dollars which the whole distance from Buffalo to New York would cost. The exit for both directions joined up at the same control, and only a ticket could be accepted to back a lower charge. . .

Back in New York the Ford unfortunately had to be returned. Rico went back to Europe. The Siffert Racing Team set about finding a car to get them to Mexico. After visiting a good number of secondhand car dealers on the outskirts of New York, Joseph found at last an old Pontiac for 1200 dollars. Luckily the vendor was accommodating — an agreement was signed whereby Seppi would pay 200 dollars down and the remainder of the price would be discussed when they got back.

Before taking the road to Mexico Joseph tried to do a deal with a petrol company to pay for the fuel for the journey. Finally, by Telex from London, BP who were not represented in America but with whom Seppi already had a small contract in Europe, agreed to reimburse the petrol bills.

Then the caravan got going: New York, Kansas, Denver, Colorado, Grand Canyon, Nevada, California, San Diego and Mexico. Seppi, Paul, Jean-Pierre and Heini covered nearly 7500 miles in fifteen days. They took turns to drive and to read the map: Seppi and Heini, Paul and Jean-Pierre. Only one night in two was spent in a motel, the other was passed clocking up the miles.

The journey was hard work but it was relieved by a fund of funny or spicy stories. At Indianapolis and at Riverside Seppi and his friends were allowed a few laps on the circuits; at Las Vegas Paul, who was not yet twenty, was refused admission to the Casino. The countryside changed, their experiences accumulated, only the menu never varied: hamburger, cornflakes, milk.

In Mexico the team was nearly lynched by a village stirred up by the hotel keeper when Seppi refused to pay the hotel bill on which the prices had been doubled during the night. One morning, 40 miles from Mexico City, Siffert went to sleep at the wheel and walloped the pavement; the car could not go on. Together with Paul, he went into Mexico by bus to find a secondhand wheel together with a crowd of Mexicans who were going to sell their produce in the market.

In Mexico, the four Swiss found by good luck a small motel, quite cheap, with a swimming pool, situated not far from the motor circuit at Mixhuca Magdalena. But they had very little time to rest: they had to repair the gearbox which had lost a tooth at Watkins Glen, and prepare the Lotus for the Grand Prix which Siffert finished in ninth position — which was worth much more to him than the 200 dollars starting money he had been paid.

With only one invitation, Group Siffert naturally arrived in force at the dinner held the evening after the race and distinguished itself by its noble appetite! The next day the team took the road again back to America, going this time through New Orleans, Texas and Washington, and arrived in

New York only a few hours before their plane left. Joseph did not have time to bargain over the price for the Pontiac, and in the end he gave it back to its owner for 450 dollars less than the agreed price. The car had cost exactly the same amount as he had won in the Mexican Grand Prix.

Their arrival in Fribourg did not pass unnoticed: Joseph and Paul descended from the train wearing immense Mexican hats as Jean-Pierre and Heini had remained in London to bring back the Lotus by road.

A bit marginal on the financial side, the expedition had been a great success in the realm of public relations. The Siffert Racing Team was from now on recognized in the world of motor racing as a serious independent team, and not as a bunch of amateurs. The Association of Grand Prix Drivers underlined this after their acceptance of Joseph and voted him the Wolfgang von Trips Memorial Trophy which was to reward the best independent driver and the one who had shown most merit during the previous season.

For Joseph, who would not compete in the last Grand Prix of the year, in South Africa, the 1963 season was over. But already he was thinking about 1964. The Lotus 23 was not all that competitive and Siffert hesitated about placing an order with Colin Chapman. The efforts of the Lotus works had been concentrated on the world champion, Jim Clark. So Seppi accepted Rico Steinemann's proposition to buy a chassis from Brabham Repco — whom the Zurich journalist had already been representing for some time. But the car could not be delivered in time for the beginning of the season, so Joseph would have to carry on for a bit with the Lotus. But in the meantime, there was the winter during which he would have to stock up his funds . . .

* * * * *

The 1964 season began for Joseph on the 14th April at

Syracuse where he would have liked to repeat his victory of the year before. Alain Zurcher, a friend from Geneva, joined him for the trip. In practice on the Saturday Seppi made a mistake rounding the last corner before the grandstand: the Lotus climbed onto the straw bales and turned over before coming to a standstill on the track. Half thrown out, Seppi was trapped inside the car when it fell back on the circuit. Held prisoner in the cockpit, the driver could not breathe: a piece of Plexiglass from the windscreen was pressing against his throat. Petrol was dripping everywhere.

Quickly pulled clear, Siffert was laid out a few feet away from the single-seater. During this time, Jean-Pierre and Alain, who had realised what had happened, had run through the stands towards the scene of the accident. When they got there they were reassured to hear Seppi's voice: 'Jean-Pierre! The car — how is it?'

'Not good,' replied the mechanic, who had not even glanced at it.

'You must get it repaired quick. Tomorrow I've got to be on the start-line,' said the injured driver whom a doctor was checking over on the spot with a stethoscope.

A full diagnosis at the Syracuse hospital revealed a cracked collarbone, bad abrasions all over his back and the right cheek badly cut. The car was more or less intact: only the front suspension and the windscreen were broken.

Siffert then found himself wrapped in an enormous bandage on which was inscribed: 'Do not remove before the 5th May.' Seppi could not take this sort of delay and demanded to see the X-rays. The doctor told him that for him the only remedy was patience and after a week of quiet he would be able to go back to Switzerland.

'You can't think that I'm going to stay for a whole week here,' thought Joseph, who told himself that willpower was a healing factor just as valuable as patience!

Then the procession of visitors began. It seemed as if the

whole of Sicily wanted to offer sympathy to last year's victor — to such a point that at midnight Jean-Pierre and Alain had their hands full to make the visitors leave. The same invasion started again on Sunday with one important caller in addition: Rob Walker, whose private team was the most celebrated in the automobile world.

On Monday morning, at four o'clock, Jean-Pierre and Alain penetrated the hospital like a pair of thieves and started a thorough kidnapping of Seppi with the sole difference that the victim was a consenting one and had himself established the plan. From there the robbers and their hostage made their way to the airport and waited for the plane, like perfect gentlemen.

Back in Fribourg, Joseph made a short stay in hospital, then he took up his commercial activities again. Having moved with Sabine to the Rue Reichlen, he set up a small office there and each morning with David Raymond he would plan the day's operations, telephoning his eventual customers and the vendors and organizing rendezvous. Joseph Siffert was no longer an exclusively travelling salesman.

The 2nd May found Siffert on the starting grid of the Daily Express Trophy Race at Silverstone in which he finished eleventh with the Lotus patched up and, as he thought, making its last appearance with Siffert at the wheel: the Brabham should be delivered next weekend for Monaco.

But the chasis still was not ready and he had to drive the Lotus 24 at Monaco; it had become so out-of-date now that he just couldn't qualify on his own. Jack Brabham then gave him a tow in his slipstream for 25 laps and he managed a time good enough to put him on the grid among the 18 starters.

The Brabham was finally delivered at Zandvoort for the Dutch Grand Prix but it took a long time to set up, and Seppi ended the race thirteenth. On top of this he only managed to pay for the car after scraping the bottom of the barrel; he made every economy he could, or rather, the last economies

Poised for the Casino corner in the Monaco Grand Prix of 1969 in which he came third

Committed driver: the Tecno in the Temporada series of 1968

Victory with Brian Redman in the 1000-kilometre race at Nurburgring in spite of a damaged right stabili[sing] wing

Flying Le Mans start with the Porsche 908 in the 24-hour race, 1969

left because in the meantime he had bought a van which could transport two cars and their spares — and a Formula Two Brabham.

Seppi wanted to develop his team. On the 9th June he held a press conference during which a new look for the Siffert Racing Team was officially announced; two drivers: Joseph Siffert and Franz Dorfliger — from Balsthal in the Solothurn, who had competed in a number of Formula Junior races during the Argentine Temporada series in 1963; a manager, Paul Blancpain; three mechanics — Heini Mader, Jean-Pierre Oberson and Claude Maradan; four cars — a van, two trailers and a petrol contract with BP. Not everything went well: Siffert had to retire in the Belgian Grand Prix; in the French Grand Prix at Rouen he burst the engine in the last practice and Tim Parnell lent him another — but he had to retire after two laps, so that he could only claim the starting money and that was that.

There were two races the following weekend at Reims: the 12-hour race which started at midnight and in the afternoon a Formula Two race. Siffert took part in both. On checking the circuit, Paul suggested that Seppi, usually well back, should go out in front from the start of practice. Seppi agreed and from that day he always tried to start first. The noise of the first car never goes unnoticed; Siffert realized that his red helmet with the white cross was beginning to get noticed, and made it clear to the organizers that here was a team that meant business.

At the Grand prix de la Solitude at Stuttgart, the set-up was just the same as the year before; the financial situation was dicey and an engine written off could finish the whole Siffert Racing Team. It was raining at the start and on the first lap a pile-up knocked out the cars of Brabham, Hill and Bandini. Joseph drove badly; for once he just couldn't press on. But he finished seventh all the same, behind Bob Anderson.

The launching of a register of supporters for the Siffert Racing Team soon after the press conference had not achieved the hoped-for results. In spite of the devoted labours of Jo Pasquier, the Fribourg financiers and captains of industry mostly turned a deaf ear and only the real friends put up their meagre contributions. Once again, Siffert could see that he would have to go it alone and that courage, perseverance and willpower were not enough unless fortune smiled as well.

His luck turned a fortnight later at the Nurburgring and Seppi took a fourth place in the German Grand Prix and three points in the Championship. Hope was re-born. The next week the Swiss driver set off with Guy von der Weid, Paul Blancpain and Paul Taramarca, the Swiss aerobatic champion, to compete in the Schauinsland hill-climb near Freiburg-im-Breisgau, at the wheel of a works Ford Cobra lent by Carroll Shelby. He came in third. On the way back Guy, who was driving a much more powerful car, could not shake off Seppi, who would catch up on the corners the time he lost on the straights. Beside him Taramarca was white as a sheet. When they got back to Fribourg he remained sitting in the car, quite rigid. He had locked both his hands under his seat during the journey and now he was literally stuck in his seat, unable to move!

The publicity given to motor racing in Switzerland at this time did not amount to very much. The papers did of course cover the main races and they talked of the rising young Fribourg star, but only the fans were interested. With no circuit racing on Swiss soil, the public could not really get worked up over competition abroad. With the idea of stirring up a bit more attention for his activities, Siffert would telephone me every so often, at the end of practice or after a race, to keep me posted on what races he was entered for and how he was doing. I would write a short report for the press agency *Sportinformation*.

Before leaving for the Mediterranean Grand Prix at Enna, Seppi was a bit hesitant: 'It's an awful job telephoning from Sicily, so I won't call you unless I win,' he told me with a laugh.

Wednesday evening the telephone rang: 'I've beaten Clark in the first practice,' Seppi told me.

'Well done. Try and keep the best time for the start of the race,' I told him, without thinking too much of it. After all, Clark was the reigning World Champion.

The next day the telephone rang again: 'Nobody has done better than me — I've got pole for tomorrow — with Clark beside me!'

This time I sat up. Sunday seemed to last for ever. Finally the radio put me out of my misery with an announcement that couldn't fail to rejoice the hearts of all sporting Swiss: in the lead for 58 out of 60 laps, Joseph Siffert had won the Mediterranean Grand Prix at Enna in 1 hour 17 minutes and 59.3 seconds at a record average speed of 221.899 kilometres an hour, or over 138 mph, beating Jim Clark by a tenth of a second!

For the first time in the history of motor racing an independent had beaten the world champion in a Formula One epreuve. To the journalist who questioned him afterwards, Clark replied with a grin: 'Siffert went too fast!'

The telephone was a long time ringing. Finally towards 9 o'clock in the evening Paul called me and confirmed the news. The victory was worthily celebrated. Brandy flowed in rivers. Tim Parnell saw Jean-Pierre absolutely plastered, hatchet in hand, explaining that he wished to split the jukebox in half because he did not like the music . . .

The European season drew to an end: only the Austrian and Italian Grands Prix were left — and the motor car Tour de France in which Siffert would take part with David Piper on a Ferrari GTA — then the Formula One circus would take off for America. Joseph could only get the same starting money as last year and he felt inclined not to enter. Jo Bonnier, the President of the GPDA, suggested to Rob Walker for whom he was driving that he could sign up the Swiss for the two transatlantic races. A friend of Seppi's since 1961, Jo Bonnier had often helped Seppi to resolve his problems: he had faith in him.

'Only talent and an iron will are enough to make a champion. Siffert has always had both these qualities, and I knew at once that he had a future in motor sport,' so Bonnier said later. It was through Bonnier that Seppi met the sculptor-engineer Jean Tinguely, already well known in Switzerland for the celebrated *Eureka* which he had exhibited in Lausanne that year. Tinguely was a passionate devotee of racing, and the two men rapidly became friends.

Rob Walker hesitated. He had already signed up Hap Sharp to drive in the United States Grand Prix. Bonnier suggested that the Brabham need only be painted in Rob's colours and he could enter it. The English patron agreed. He hardly knew Seppi, whom he had visited after his accident in Syracuse and whom he had bumped into on the circuit, but nothing more.

On its arrival at Watkins Glen, Siffert's Brabham BRM changed colours; having always been red, it now became dark blue with a white band in front. The race was a success; Siffert came third, gaining four extra points in the world championship. Unfortunately things went less well with Mexico where he had to retire with engine trouble.

Rob Walker was pleased. He had decided to run two cars in 1965, why not Siffert? But the young Jochen Rindt was also interested in running for Rob Walker whose colours he had carried in the last Austrian Grand Prix and who was often in touch on the telephone. Rob was undecided. Both men were good. Seppi was not yet very well known, but at least he was known. Rindt however had made a start in Formula One and he had a much better chance of finding another team; the Cooper factory had already made him an offer.

So Rob Walker made his choice of a second driver for 1965 to run as number two to Jo Bonnier in the person of Jo Siffert. And he also took on the two mechanics and bought up all the spare parts.

Seppi was at last taken care of. Paul would remain on the sidelines but he would be mainly occupied with the commercial side which Seppi would now be able to expand independently of his motor racing.

CHAPTER FIVE

Joseph's commercial activities during the winter were interrupted by his taking part in his first South African Grand Prix, the 1st January 1965 at East London, where he finished seventh. His next epreuve was not until some two and a half months later, at Brands Hatch. He was entered for the traditional Race of Champions there, which every year marks the opening of the European Formula One season.

Heini and Jean-Pierre were installed in England at Dorking in Surrey, the headquarters of the Rob Walker Racing Team. Rob now knew Seppi a great deal better. It was the first time in a long career that the motor racing patron had taken on a driver who was not well known — or at least not yet. Not that he minded — on the contrary; for the first time he had a driver who would listen to his advice. And Rob could pass on to him the benefit of his considerable experience built up when Stirling Moss was driving for him. A mutual understanding was soon built up between Rob and Seppi; each was anxious to help the other.

At Syracuse where his memories were either happy or sad, depending on whether he thought of his victory in 1963 or his accident in 1964, Seppi listened closely to the words of Rob Walker. 'On these fast circuits where you generally get a tight pack in front, Stirling would keep just ahead, then, if a small gap occurred when lapping back markers he would force the pace through the next corners, which would often have the effect of cracking the pursuit's morale and leave them to fight over second place.'

The race was exciting. Running on rails, Siffert and Surtees swopped the lead continually. Fifty yards behind them, Jim Clark followed without mixing it with them. After 40 laps, they started overtaking the back markers, among them Jo Bonnier — Rob signalled him the position: Siffert, Surtees, Clark. Bonnier understood. Seppi passed him in front of the stands just before a tricky corner at the end, which was difficult and in any case impossible to take flat out. A good team-mate, the Swedish driver lifted his foot for a moment, obliging Surtees and Clark to do the same. In front, Seppi remembered Rob's words; he pushed ahead and built up a small, but sufficient, lead on his rivals who did not try to catch him. Victory was almost in the bag. Ten laps from the end, however, going over a small bump, fifth gear jumped out; the revs of Seppi's BRM engine shot sky-high and it blew up. Siffert retired. Surtees took the lead but his engine failed two laps later, and Jim Clark won the race.

'It was a fantastic fight, but I just didn't want to know with Seppi and Big John [a nickname for Surtees] dicing together side by side through the corners at 140 mph!' Jimmy told Rob after the race as they drove back to their hotel.

Rob Walker was very happy: Seppi's incredible drive reminded him very much of the great Stirling Moss . . .

Traditionally there is always a meeting at Goodwood on Easter Monday. Seppi was confident. Without being quite up to the works machines, his Brabham was running beautifully; the suspension had been revised and several improvements made as a result of practical experience in competition. The Swiss driver started badly but he moved rapidly up through the field from sixteenth to sixth place, then suddenly, going through the chicane — already made famous by Hawthorn and Behra who had both tangled it there — the back wheel of the Brabham hit the wall at 75 mph; the car spun round and crashed head on into the other wall. The safety squad moved in immediately and first of all switched off the ignition to reduce the risk of fire — Seppi's main worry — and then pulled him clear, half unconscious. He was taken to the first aid tent and then straight to hospital. His right leg was broken and his face was terribly swollen. The slightest movement brought on a frightful pain in his back. At the Royal West Hospital in Chichester, the X-rays showed some damage to the vertebrae of his spine.

After a week at Chichester, Siffert could be taken home. Alain Zurcher took charge of him at Geneva Airport and drove him to Fribourg to the Garcia Clinic where the Doctors Gonzague de Meyer and Paul Martin prescribed in the first place absolute rest.

Resigned, and not too downhearted, Seppi did as he was told. For the first time in his life, he read a book — on motor racing naturally!

One morning a Swiss television company came to interview him; Joseph longed to see himself on the small screen. He commissioned me and Jo Pasquier to find a television set and install it in his room at the hospital. The set was easily hired; much more difficult, an aerial was then borrowed from the store of one of the Fribourg dealers.

His injuries soon mended; he certainly did not miss any chance to accelerate the process. No sooner had the doctors told him that milk was good for the recalcification of the bones than Seppi literally gorged himself with cheese and even yoghourt which he detested. One day he asked Claude Maradan to leave his car outside the Clinic, and he escaped for a whole afternoon. At the little office which he had been renting for some time in the Rue du Simplon, his sister Theresa and David couldn't believe their eyes when they saw him arriving — albeit somewhat stiffly.

In England, Jean-Pierre and Heini worked flat out to set up a new chassis which Rob Walker had ordered from Brabham as soon as he knew that Seppi would almost certainly be back on his feet for the Belgian Grand Prix.

In fact, Joseph was back on the road, or said that he was, a fortnight before the Monaco Grand Prix which was run exactly six weeks after Goodwood. On this occasion the official programme referred to him as Jo Siffert: it was true that Joseph was rather a long name for a man who went so fast! Strapped into a corset and with his right leg still bandaged, Siffert managed to qualify though not without some pain. Seppi tried to hide it, but Rob was watching and asked him if he really wanted to race.

'It'll be difficult, but I think I can make it,' he replied.

His forecast to his friend, Lucien Balsiger, was not quite so optimistic: 'This bloody track is all accelerating and braking — it hurts like hell, and I don't think I can keep going for more than twenty laps.' Formula One cars did not have servo-assisted brakes!

Siffert did start, all the same. In the scramble on the first run past the Casino, he was suddenly baulked by another car and had to brake so hard that the pain made him think for a moment that he had broken his leg again. Very uncomfortable in his corset, anyone could see that he was in pain and his friends hoped that he would come in. But he went on. By the fiftieth lap out of the hundred which make up the race, he was right in it. As the laps mounted he seemed to get more red in the face. His agony didn't finish until he saw the chequered flag waved by Louis Chiron, the Race Director. Jo Siffert finished in sixth place — which brought him one point in the world championship — and two laps behind Jackie Stewart, the winner, but only four seconds behind Bruce McLaren who was fifth.

Exhausted and a bit groggy, he couldn't get himself out of the car without help. Almost apologising, he spoke to Rob Walker: 'If my leg hadn't hurt so much, I would certainly have taken McLaren!'

After massage treatment, Seppi flew the next day to England and on the Wednesday he joined Georges and Josianne Blanc at Cavaillon. Two days later, he came first in the hill-climb at Mont-Ventoux on a Formula Two Brabham, which brought him in a thousand francs and a bouquet of flowers which he presented to Josianne.

Eighth in the Belgian Grand Prix, Siffert then found himself driving in the Le Mans 24-Hour Race in an enormous 5-litre Maserati, which he shared with Jochen Nerpasch, entered by Colonel Simone. Too powerful and not very well prepared, the car did not have much of a chance of finishing.

Joseph however distinguished himself by his dashing start; when other entrants were only just starting up, the Maserati was already off down the track. Forgetting his weak leg, and the fragile state of his back, Seppi ran fastest of all to the car and hopped in with a subtle skill. The 24-Hours of Le Mans only lasted 15 minutes: on the third lap Siffert went off the road and fetched up in the sand at Tertre Rouge.

Monsieur Georges Pompidou, then the French Prime Minister, was present at Clermont-Ferrand for the Grand Prix of the Automobile Club de France. Before the race the drivers were all presented to him, but after he had shaken hands with Jo Siffert, he was interrupted by Jo Pasquier: 'Excuse me, Monsieur Pompidou, but would you mind shaking hands with Siffert again because I would like to take a photograph.'

The Prime Minister smiled and agreed. Staggered, not by his own temerity, but by the courtesy of the Minister, Jo Pasquier forgot to take a picture. 'I didn't dare ask him to do it for a third time!' he told me.

Often gauche or flippant, the Group Siffert did not bother with the finer points of language or behaviour. Their attitude — simple, natural and straightforward — sometimes made people laugh, or sympathise with them. Seppi felt much more at ease in his black leather jacket than he did in a dinner jacket — though he looked quite well in one — because that usually meant that he was in the company of people whom he did not know how to address. Adopting a formula which seemed to him quite logical, he produced a timid 'Bonjour Monsieur le Prince' for Prince Napoleon, when he was presented to him one day in Geneva. The lessons in conduct and good manners of his old master of apprentices, Carlo Frangi, had not foreseen just this eventuality!

Public relations were all important. I couldn't help noticing one day when Seppi missed a chance to get his own back on someone of whom he was not over-fond. 'It's only the mountains which can't move to meet each other,' he said.

The development of the business took precedence over everything else except racing. Not long before, the Fribourg Commune had leased to Siffert a site on the outskirts of the town going in the direction of Bulle. Joseph had built there a prefabricated showroom and two sales offices. Another stage surmounted. An enormous illuminated sign was fixed up outside reading 'Joseph Siffert Automobiles'. Seppi was quite proud of his achievement. David Raymond and Paul Blancpain looked after the sales; Claude Maradan was responsible for the workshop at the Mouret Forge; the office in the Rue du Simplon was transformed into an auto-boutique run by his sister Adelaide and, on and off, by his mother or Theresa.

The 15th August 1965 Jo Siffert was once again on the grid for the Mediterranean Grand Prix at Enna. As the year before he had pole position with Jim Clark beside him. The Scots driver had not yet won the world championship, but unofficially he already was the champion and nobody could beat him after his victory in Germany a fortnight before.

The two of them provided the spectacle — right through the race Seppi and Jimmy passed and re-passed, sometimes five times in a lap, on the circuit round the lake at Enna-Pergusa. The Brabham was less powerful than the works Lotus of Clark, so Siffert had to perform prodigies not to be shaken off and to keep in the running. Going through some sections by the pits, the tail of the car was hung out so far that Rob Walker was afraid he would hit the opposite wall of the track. On the last lap Joseph went through in front and then Jim took him just after the stands. The Swiss gave up the attack. Then, in the last corner, he gambled the lot and changed down a gear! The rev counter leapt wildly, the engine screamed, but it held. Siffert overtook Clark and for the second time running he beat him — this time by three-tenths of a second at an average speed of 224.051 kilometres an hour, improving on his own record speed of the year before.

Jim Clark's grin was a little less pronounced than the year before: 'Siffert was so broadside on that I didn't know whether I ought to take him on the left or the right!' he commented to the journalists.

In the Siffert camp the excitement was terrific. It was the first victory for the Rob Walker Racing Team since Stirling Moss had won the German Grand Prix in 1961. Rob Walker was walking on air. He was convinced now that Seppi was one of the great drivers — and he never had reason to change his mind.

Franco Lini, the Italian journalist, was also delighted for Joseph whom he had picked out in Cesenatico in 1961: 'With all these victories you've carried off,' he said laughing, 'you ought to come and live in Sicily — it must be your sort of country!'

Another first place was waiting for Siffert the next weekend — this time in Switzerland — the Sainte Ursanne to Les Rangiers hill-climb in which Seppi was driving a Brabham BRM.

In the world of motor racing, the discussions were at last getting somewhere: at the end of the season, the engine capacity for Formula One would go up from 1½-litres to 3-litres — the private drivers and teams asked themselves how

108

they would be able to cope. The chassis would have to be revised as well and the total costs looked like going up enormously.

In the car taking them from Geneva to Les Rangiers, Rob Walker and Jo Bonnier discussed the problems which would soon be upon them.

'What do you think you will do next year?' asked Bonnier.

'I can't run two cars, it will be too expensive: so I shall only need one driver.'

'Yes — and which?'

'Seppi, I think.'

Thoughtful and courteous, Rob Walker had to say this to Bonnier. 'It was fair,' he told me later. 'Seppi was the better.'

Joachim Bonnier didn't at all want to stay: he understood that Rob preferred to have a younger driver, talented and aggressive, with a future.

Bonnier and Siffert always remained on the best of the terms and talked of starting an Ecurie Suisse for Formulas One and Two during the next season.

Eleventh at Watkins Glen, Joseph collected three more points for the Drivers' World Championship in Mexico and he ended the year eleventh in the Championship listing with five points.

Jo Siffert now made a firm commitment for the next season: he would continue under the colours of the Rob Walker Racing Team in 1966, driving a V12 Cooper-Maserati which would be delivered at the beginning of the new season. As Rob would now only have one driver, he also had to reduce the number of mechanics. Heini Mader and Jean-Pierre Oberson had to go, but their first-class reputations did not leave them without work for long, and Bonnier soon signed them up for the team he had just founded.

Although he didn't go looking for prizes, Siffert appreciated them when they were deserved. His victory over Jim Clark at Enna should have earned him the highest annual award for a racing driver in Switzerland, the President of the Automobile Club Cup.

Joseph was, however, overlooked. By way of protest, Rico Steinemann and the Swiss journalists who specialized in motor sport organized a BP racing trophy and nominated Siffert as it first recipient; it was solemnly presented to him in Zurich by the journalist Ernst Graf.

* * * * *

The South African Grand Prix of 1966 traditionally held on the 1st January for once did not count for the Drivers' World Championship. There were not many of the new 3-litre engines ready, and certainly not enough of them for the race to be properly homologated. Driving his Brabham with a 2-litre BRM engine, which had just run in the Tasman Series, Siffert got a good second place behind Mike Spence.

Seppi, who had completely given up smoking for a year, dreamt of becoming more and more professional and taking part in the maximum number of races. He no longer had the financial worries of an independent driver; from now on the sporting side would become more essential to him and dealing receded in importance. 'I am only really happy when I'm racing,' he would always say.

But to race you have to have contracts. In Zurich, Charles Voegele, a driver of something over forty was looking for a co-driver to compete with him in his new Porsche Carrera 6 in some of the endurance races counting for the Sports Car Manufacturers' World Championship. Rico Steinemann suggested that he should ask Siffert, who accepted immediately.

The two Swiss took part in their first event together when, on the 25th March, they competed in the Sebring 12-Hour Race in which they finished sixth.

For Formula Two, Siffert joined the Ecurie Suisse which the Automobile Club Suisse, the governing body of motor

110

sport in Switzerland, looked on with a jaundiced eye. But the Cooper-BRM with which they provided him was not very well set up; at Pau he failed to start, and his seventh place at Goodwood involved a good deal of hard work.

The management of the Porsche works had registered the talent and skill that Jo Siffert had demonstrated on the 25th April, in the Monza 1000-Kilometre Race; Ferdinand Piech, the engineer, a nephew of Ferdinand Porsche, even thought that the Swiss driver would be a useful reinforcement for the works team, but Baron Huschke von Hanstein, Porsche racing director, was more sceptical.

In Formula One, the Rob Walker Racing Team had just taken delivery of the 3-litre Cooper-Maserati, but it proved a very difficult car to set up. Siffert retired at Syracuse, in the International Trophy Race at Silverstone and at Monaco.

For the 1000-Kilometre Race at the Nurburgring, Ferdinand Piech, with the agreement of Charles Voegele, asked Siffert to try a few laps on a works Porsche; if he was needed, and if his times were better than those of the other drivers, the Swiss might be given a works machine. Seppi only turned in the same lap times as his opponents and his chance to uphold the Stuttgart works colours was knocked on the head when Baron von Hanstein brought over by air at the last moment the Sicilian driver Nino Vaccarella. Siffert ran with Voegele in the Porsche Carrera 6 but they were soon out of the race with engine trouble.

The next day, Ferdinand Piech took up Joseph's cause with his cousin Ferry Porsche, who gave him a free hand. Siffert was summoned to Stuttgart soon afterwards where he signed a contract for the next endurance race, this time the Le Mans 24-Hour Race.

The problems with the Cooper-Maserati were not resolved by a long way for the Belgian Grand Prix at Spa on the following Sunday, when the two Walker team mechanics, Tony Cleverley and Nick Dole had to work all out. Rob had only bought this very heavy car because there wasn't anything else on the market. Seppi handled it well and its good roadholding allowed him to hang on to the faster cars. But the engine, which never realized its full potential power, was not at all robust, and often broke down. The trickiest problem was the cooling; it overheated so badly during the weekend at Spa that the car could not complete one lap.

'Let's hope it rains,' said Seppi, who did not at all like running in the rain, but realized that it could do something for him — in the wet he might be able to get his truck to keep up with somebody or other slowed down by a slippery track.

He got his wish and the track was soaking when the race started. Siffert however was rapidly forced to retire after a shunt. But Rob Walker was happy at last: honour was saved, for the Cooper-Maserati had accomplished more than one lap and Seppi was all right. Rob had always had a horror of racing in the rain; he was so pleased to see his young driver safe and sound that he didn't mind about the retirement at all. 'The result doesn't matter,' he said to Georges Blanc. 'Seppi is still there.'

The first race in which Jo Siffert competed as an official Porsche works driver was a success; with Colin Davis as co-driver, the Swiss took fourth place in the final overall classification in the 1966 Le Mans 24-Hour Race, and won the Index of Performance — based on the distance run in relation to the cylinder capacity of the car.

At the beginning of July, Joseph managed to forget his latest retirement with the Cooper-Maserati in the French Grand Prix at Reims, celebrating his thirtieth birthday. Sabine and their friends had organized a superb party in his honour at Granges-Paccot.

But the disappointments were not over; he had to retire in the British Grand Prix at Brands Hatch and in the Dutch Grand Prix at Zandvoort. For the Nurburgring, Seppi was fed-up; for the third time in fourteen years Rob Walker

Airborne in the 1969 German Grand Prix at Nurburgring

The March at Mor

The Porsche 917 at
Daytona Beach in

Jo Siffert attacks in
Can-Am Porsche

refused to enter a car; his motive was financial — the starting money offered by the organizers would not even cover the outgoings.

'I don't ask much, but I don't race for almost nothing,' said Rob. His decision was final.

Joseph found some consolation in the Les Rangiers hill-climb where his Cooper-Maserati enabled him to repeat his victory of the year before.

The large numbers of Swiss spectators who go each year to Monza were also disappointed; Siffert retired on the 47th lap with engine trouble. In Switzerland, the public started to ask themselves: is Siffert a car-breaker? The motoring journalists knew that he wasn't that at all, and they said so. But the non-enthusiasts no longer believed in him. And this, although Seppi demonstrated his talent on any occasion that the mechanical means at his disposal allowed him. He came second in the Austrian Grand Prix, which was run for the first time this year, on a works Porsche.

The Cooper-Maserati managed to finish a race at last at Watkins Glen in the United States Grand Prix where Siffert chalked up his only three points of the season; he came fourteenth in the World Championship, which was won this year by Brabham.

The Swiss driver's score-sheet for the season was not very brilliant. It should be pointed out, of course, that 1966 was a season of transition. The new regulations for Formula One engines had to be tested out. A private enterprise, the Walker team never got the hoped-for technical and mechanical assistance on which they had counted.

Joseph did not take on too much. His contract with Rob Walker had been renewed for 1967. With Porsche he became more and more their front-line works driver, and his programme for next year meant that he would drive in all the events counting for the two World Championships — the Formula One Drivers' and the Sports Car Constructors'. For

Formula Two, Siffert had also got a works contract with BMW who had decided to make a come-back into competition work. In this list, Formula One of course would take precedence, then the Sports Car Constructors' Championship, and Formula Two last.

The interval between seasons was short; Siffert had barely two months for his commercial activities. Jo Bonnier invited him to Begnins near Geneva for Christmas Eve, where he took on the role of Father Christmas for all the village children.

* * * * *

Things became more serious again on the 2nd January 1967 at Kyalami in South Africa, where Joseph's Cooper-Maserati was still a disappointment; the clutch failed on the 36th lap. A month later, for the 24-Hour Race at Daytona Beach in Florida, sharing the wheel with the German driver Hans Herrmann, Siffert took fourth place — all the more satisfactory as the factory were running for the first time the new Porsche 910 which would replace the Carrera. Originally a baker, his team-mate was a veteran with many years of competition experience which was an invaluable standby.

The BMW T100 made its first appearance at Silverstone in a Formula Two race; the car, however, was still in the middle of its teething troubles.

Race followed race, one much the same as the next; Jo Siffert did not finish in any Formula race except the French Grand Prix raced this year at Le Mans where he came in fourth.

Heavy, without being very strong, complete with twelve cylinders but no power, the Cooper-Maserati just wasn't competitive.

Things went much better for the Sports Car Constructors' Championship and Seppi became a real master in this type of

114

racing; the small engine capacity of the Porsche 910 did not let him carry off the endurance races, but he did show exceptional skill. Fifth in the Le Mans 24-Hour Race, with Hans Herrmann as co-driver, he again won the Index of Performance.

Before leaving Reims where he had come second, with David Piper, in the 12-Hour Race on a Ferrari 330/P3, Seppi — who had brought his mother — suggested exchanging cars with Georges Blanc as far as Dijon; the racing driver would take over Georges's Cadillac and would entrust him with the Ferrari GTB. In spite of running out of petrol, Joseph and his mother got to the Hotel de la Cloche way before Georges and Josianne could catch them up.

Quiet, courteous and always discreet, Georges Blanc was perhaps Seppi's greatest friend — a little like the brother he had never had and to whom he could confide all his troubles. Private worries as well as the ordinary problems of a racing driver. Georges Blanc, who dealt in Cadillacs and lorries in the Vaud, gave good clear advice and Joseph, a few years younger, would usually act upon it.

At Silverstone, for the British Grand Prix, Franco Lini who had given up journalism to run the Ferrari team was in trouble; Lorenzo Bandini had been killed at Monaco in May, and Ludvico Scarfiotti wasn't really in the running because Formula One was not at all his thing. There was only the New Zealander, Chris Amon, to represent the flying horse of Maranello in the Italian Grand Prix at Monza, less than two months away.

Seppi was interested; could he at last get his hands on a machine worthy of his talent; Rob was quite prepared to release his protege for the one race.

However, before they got to an agreement, Enzo Ferrari vetoed the idea, maintaining that his fans would not like the Ferrari colours to be upheld by two foreigners. 'But if Amon or Siffert were to win the Italian Grand Prix, they would like it very much,' Franco Lini suggested. But in vain. The Commendatore refused to take the risk.

It was during this time that Seppi got to know well Bernard Blancpain, the uncle of Paul, and owner of the well-known Cardinal Brewery in Fribourg. From the start the friendship flourished. Bernard had raced himself before the war under the pseudonym of Macado. Without being a great champion he was nevertheless, with his friend, Toulo de Graffenried, one of the better drivers in the years 1937 and 1938. In 1939 he was really hooked and decided to leave his job as an engineer in the brewery where his father and uncles disapproved of his sporting activities. Then came the war; racing came to a stop and the brewery needed him. By the end of the war, Bernard Blancpain was married, with three children. Delage offered him a works contract for five Grands Prix. Maserati on the other hand offered him special terms. His reputation was not tremendous, but he was certainly good. In 1947, at Marseilles, Enrico Plate tempted him with a blown 1500 Maserati. Bernard hesitated. He only had to say yes. Finally, his wife grabbed him by his coat-tails and he turned the offer down. The car, which had been offered him, went on to win the epreuve all the same.

With the conviction that motor sport must be practised and that nothing is more boring than just watching a motor race, Macado withdrew altogether from the sport, almost with a reaction against it. Then, Siffert appeared and Paul's uncle was delighted to hear about the young beginner, though he did not take an active interest. In 1965 he met Siffert for the first time; two years later, taken by his character, Bernard Blancpain became a friend of Seppi and took up again his love of motor racing. And Joseph always enjoyed dropping in to the Brewery to talk over the problems with the veteran driver, thirty years older than he. And in the end, it was the same as with Georges Blanc: a real and lasting friendship sprang up between Seppi and Bernard.

Jo Siffert won his only victory of the 1967 season on the 20th August in a hill-climb. For the third year running, but at the wheel of his Formula Two BMW this time, he put in fastest time over the five kilometres Sainte Ursanne to Les Rangiers in the Swiss Jura and set up a new outright record for the run.

Then bad luck set in again; in Canada he failed to qualify and he retired once again at Monza. At Watkins Glen, however, he finished fourth which led to some unkind stories that the lure of dollars had made his foot a little more gentle and so allowed the Cooper-Maserati to keep going to the end of the race!

Coming in twelfth in Mexico Siffert ended the Drivers' World Championship in eleventh place with six points. During this last race, Rob Walker and Franco Lini watched the way Seppi completely mastered the Cooper-Maserati: 'It's extraordinary how much he reminds me of Stirling Moss,' Rob said to Franco — who had not let Seppi's poor results over the season impress him too much. Seppi's quality as a driver was real enough — and given a good car, it was a safe bet that his talents would be enough to convince a wider audience than the experts. Tim Parnell was also well aware of this.

The Ferrari and BRM factories had both made offers to the Swiss driver, but he was still undecided: he very much wanted to stay with Porsche which would rule out a Maranello contract, and then the atmosphere of the Walker team suited him to a T; Joseph felt like part of a family. And Rob, who was not pushing him at all, wanted him to stay and was promising a good car for 1968. Finally, Seppi accepted the last offer which gave him complete freedom for the Sports Car Constructors' World Championship.

On his return to Switzerland, Siffert went almost straight off to Monza where he joined three other Swiss drivers: Charles Voegele, Dieter Spoerri and Rico Steinemann. All four of them at the wheel of a Porsche Carrera 6 Special, with assistance from the works and support from BP, were going to try and beat the world record over 15,000 kilometres, over 10,000 miles and over 72 hours, held by a Toyota 2000GT, as well as the record for 20,000 kilometres and 96 hours which had been set up by a Ford Comet. In addition, if they were successful in their main attempts, they would set up a further ten new international records.

The attempt started badly: on the evening of the 29th October after they had run over 2,000 kilometres on the Monza Speedway circuit, the Carrera broke down for good. It was then decided to start again the next day with a Porsche 911R. For four days and four nights the four drivers took turns at the wheel, completing each lap in little more than a minute, and one by one the records fell. They took the last after 96 hours during which the Porsche had run 20,000.086 kilometres at an average speed of 209.233 kilometres an hour — over 130 mph.

Whilst all this was going on, Rob Walker was trying to make up his mind; Ken Tyrell advised him to buy a Lotus, but Rob thought that they broke down a lot. Geoff Thomas, his partner, agreed with Tyrrell and suggested the same thing: 'Of all the constructors, Colin Chapman is certainly the best,' he told him.

A rendezvous in London was fixed at Prunier's where Rob proposed a deal. His garage in Somerset was doing well; Rob would like to take on the Lotus agency if Chapman would give him special terms for the acquisition of a second-hand Formula One car, followed by a new one.

The two men soon reached agreement; Chapman would sell the Lotus 49 with a new Ford engine which Jim Clark would drive in South Africa and he would supply a new chassis during the season.

Seppi was delighted and so was Rob Walker. Could his team now compete on equal terms with the works? From

118

what had been achieved in the past, it looked as if it could.

A member of the well-known Scottish whisky family and a descendant of Johnny Walker himself, Rob Walker was also once a racing driver. He competed in his first race in 1934 when he was seventeen. In 1938 he bought a Delahaye and finished eighth with it in the Le Mans 24-Hour Race of 1939. It was still the time when most racing drivers drove without helmets.

When war broke out, Rob found himself in the Fleet Air Arm and a pilot, in the Aircraft Carrier *Victorious*. When Rob proposed to Betty she accepted him only on the condition that he would give up racing, except in a straight line! Rob accepted the condition; he would only remain in racing by means of his private team which he had founded soon after the war. The Rob Walker Racing Team rapidly made a reputation for itself; it numbered several great names among its drivers – Prince Bira; Arthur Dobson; Tony Holt – Victor at Le Mans in 1953; Peter Collins; Roy Salvadori; Reg Parnell – the father of Tim; Tony Brooks – until 1957; and then Jack Brabham. At this time Stirling Moss was under contract to Vanwall for Formula One but he carried Rob's colours in Formula Two. In 1958 Maurice Trintignant won the Monaco Grand Prix for the Walker team. Moss himself won in the Argentine and from the end of the year drove exclusively for Rob. In 1959 at Aintree, the team cleaned up everything: Moss and Trintignant in Formula One, Brooks in Formula Two. In 1961 Stirling carried off the Grands Prix at Monaco and the Nurburgring.

The following year was disastrous: although Trintignant won at Pau, Moss had a serious accident at Goodwood on the same day and, as a result, had to give up active driving. In Mexico Rob gave a chance to the young Ricardo Rodriguez who was killed in practice in front of his public. Walker had entrusted his second car to an impetuous 'motard' – Gary Hocking, who had just graduated from two wheels to four.

And he, in turn, was killed in his second race. Rob Walker was terribly upset, and was almost on the point of retiring. However, he tried once more and gave a drive to Joachim Bonnier, a mature and experienced driver who would uphold the colours — blue with a white band, reminiscent of the Scottish flag — of the Rob Walker Racing Team.

CHAPTER SIX

On the 1st January 1968 Jo Siffert drove the Cooper-Maserati for the last time in the South African Grand Prix in which he finished seventh, just missing the one point for sixth place which was picked up by Beltoise on the Matra-Ford. The winner, Jim Clark, saw himself instantly dispossessed of the Lotus, which Rob Walker was going to have repainted in his colours as soon as it could be got back to England. But before Seppi could try it out, he had to go to Florida to run in the 24-Hour Race at Daytona Beach.

For the first five hours his work was cut out chasing the powerful Ford GT 40s and he had to lap faster than he had envisaged. Hounded by the small but tough 2.2-litre Porsche 907, the big 5-litre cars of Ickx/Redman and Hawkins/Hobbs were forced to retire before a third of the race had been run. From then on, Siffert took the lead and dominated the race for the remaining sixteen hours, relieved at regular intervals by Hans Herrmann. After twenty-two hours with a lead of 25 miles over the second car — Vic Elford driving an identical Porche — Siffert had to stop to have the accelerator mended — the strut had suddenly snapped. The repairs took 13 laps and the Siffert/Herrmann partnership was in second place when they rejoined the race. However, thinking that Seppi deserved to win, the Porsche team called him in, changed the names on the official entries, and let him finish the race in Elford's car. Driving alternately the two Porsches Numbers

121

52 and 53 — and apparently without a pause — Siffert and Herrmann therefore took first and second places in the Daytona Beach 24-Hour Race! The impression all this made on the Porsche racing department chief back at the factory was tremendous, and Seppi did not have too much trouble in obtaining for his Fribourg garage a second Porsche agency! Jo Siffert Automobiles would become something a bit more than a second-hand car dealer's. This new step forward meant that he could now plan a new garage, perhaps for the following year — but it would also depend on how his business and racing went during the present year.

At the beginning of March, Joseph tried the Lotus-Ford for the first time on the Brands Hatch circuit which the Walker team had hired for the purpose. At first he did not go very fast; the power of the engine came in so quick that it almost overawed him and certainly gave him a few problems. Siffert had never driven so powerful a machine! After thirty laps on the short circuit, he began to feel at home in the car, to feel a part of it; he started to increase speed and then allowed himself the luxury of equalling the lap record.

Ten days later, the traditional Race of Champions was held over the same course. So as to have the car well in hand, Siffert was running the day before official practice. The track had not been cleaned and it had rained a bit before he went out; after doing two slow laps to warm the engine up, he increased speed. At the end of the last bend before the wood, behind the pits, the Lotus skidded, walloped an observation post, bounced into the bank and came to a standstill not far away. By a miracle Siffert was not hurt, but the car was a write-off. Sadly he returned to the pits on foot and told Rob what had happened. The journalists who were there all rushed up. Joseph asked for a pencil, and then, on the badge tied to his jacket, he wrote a brief comment: *'Merde alors!'*

Rob grinned; despite the tragedy his blessed Seppi could still make a joke of it. The team went back to Dorking; Seppi returned to Switzerland whilst Rob Walker stayed at Brands Hatch to discuss with Colin Chapman how soon the new Lotus could be delivered, or the acquisition of a replacement car. The next day, during practice, Rob was called to the telephone; his manager told him that the workshops at Dorking had been completely destroyed in a fire. One of the mechanics had been working on the remains of the Lotus and a spark had started a blaze. The whole collection of old cars had been burned as well, among them the Delage, the Delahaye, the Cooper-Maserati and even the new Ford engine. Rob Walker was almost overwhelmed. The souvenirs of nearly forty years of motor sport had gone up in smoke.

That night he paid a visit to his brother-in-law in London, who asked him: 'What are you going to do?'

'I don't know,' said Rob, 'all my life I have done nothing but motor racing and the war. I don't really want to take up fighting again!'

'I'll give you fifteen thousand pounds to help you start again.'

The next day, Rob's partner, Jack Durlacher, who was also worried about what Rob would do, said that he would finance a new car. But before taking a final decision, Rob had to find out if the insurance would pay up on the £25,000 for which he was covered and which represented perhaps half the amount of the loss.

Monday morning Rob went back to Dorking where his mechanics and manager were waiting: 'We are starting again immediately,' he told them.

Next he telephoned Colin Chapman who agreed to sell him as soon as possible a Lotus and two engines which were then on their way back from Australia, where Clark had been running in the Tasman Series. Reassured, Seppi flew off again for Florida where, with Herrmann, he had an easy victory in the Sebring 12-Hour Race, the second round in the Sports Car Manufacturers' World Championship.

The next race took place on the 7th April at Brands Hatch where the Siffert/Herrmann partnership had to retire while in the lead with a locked rear wheel. On the same day, Jim Clark, the flying Scotsman, was killed at Hockenheim in a Formula Two race. The next day I met Seppi and passed him a newspaper report of the tragedy. Seppi wept. Jim Clark was not only a friend; since Joseph had twice beaten him at Enna he had become his hero, along with Benoit Musy, Raymond Sommer and Stirling Moss. 'He was the greatest of them all,' he told me, his voice choked with emotion.

Memories remain, the race goes on. The same day Joseph left for Modena where Franco Lini was determined that he should try the new Formula Two Ferrari; on Thursday the 25th April he was on the start line of the Monza 1000-Kilometre Race, driving a new 3-litre Porsche 908 which was not yet fully developed. They made numerous and lengthy stops in the pits, so the Siffert/Herrmann partnership only made nineteenth place in the final. Hardly was that race over when a second one started; Joseph had to catch a plane in Milan to get to London and then on to Silverstone where two days later he would run in the Daily Express Formula One Trophy race.

The boat carrying the Lotus from Australia did not reach England until three days before the race so Rob Walker had sent a truck and a mechanic to pick up the car in Hamburg when the boat called in there. So, in spite of the major disaster of the month before, the Rob Walker Racing Team not miss a single Formula One epreuve. The race, however, was not a success: Joseph started badly and got off the grid last. He made a spectacular comeback which took him into third place but suddenly the clutch failed and he had to retire — to the great distress of Jean-Pierre Oberson, whom Rob had just re-engaged as a mechanic in his team.

That evening Seppi landed in Geneva and together we drove to Saint Antoine near Fribourg where he had promised to run the next day, driving a 4400 cc McLaren-Oldsmobile in the hill-climb organized by the Fribourg section of the ACS. And at midnight, in the rain, we made a few ascents in the Porsche 911R; Siffert, the professional, wanted to get to know the course before running officially, thus in four days Siffert had taken part in three epreuves, one for prototypes, one for Formula One cars, plus a hill-climb. He was certainly fully occupied . . .

Seppi was not very pleased with his Lotus 49 which did not hold the road well. In practice for the Spanish Grand Prix on the Jarama circuit near Madrid his left leg was badly burned after a petrol leak in the cockpit. Although it was very painful, he started in the race all the same, saying to a friend who looked a bit worried: 'Racing is my job: if sometimes it's very hard, well, I have to take it.'

For the 1000-Kilometre race at the Nurburgring things did not augur well for him. Because of problems with the fuel-injection system Seppi only managed twenty-seventh best time in practice. On top of that, it was a Le Mans-type start — he would have to sprint across the track and jump in the car, and his burns of the week before were still painful. With Vic Elford once again as co-driver, Seppi managed to fairly bound into his Porsche and was away up the track so fast that he made up twenty-four places in one go, and tore into the first bend in third place! With the bit between his teeth, Seppi took the lead on the first lap and never let it go. He was unbeatable. In spite of the new chicane just before passing the stands, he smashed the lap record and the Siffert/Elford team lowered the total time for the race by 20 minutes, winning it comfortably.

The Lotus went better at Monaco on the following Sunday and in practice Siffert put in second best time equal with Servoz Gavin. But the gearbox seemed a bit weak, and Rob Walker ordered another to be flown out. The whole of France seemed to be on strike and the runway lights at Nice

Airport only went on in the nick of time, at midnight, to let the plane touch down. As for the Customs men, there weren't any — which made the import formalities rather easier . . .

Before the race, with Sabine, Georges Blanc and Josianne, Seppi began to get impatient when their overworked waiter took a long time producing the meal they had ordered.

'Look, I'm in a hurry,' said the racing driver. 'I'm racing this afternoon.'

'Well, monsieur, I've been racing for the last three days!' replied the waiter, with a strong Southern accent.

The race got going from the start: Servoz Gavin took the lead in front of Graham Hill and Siffert, but retired after two laps. Second, Seppi hung on to Graham but did not try to attack. The race was a long one and he had to nurse the engine. Then, on lap 12, the gearbox went and he had to retire. 'Pity,' he told me when he got back. 'If I had known I would have passed Hill and like that, I would just for once have led in a World Championship race!'

Seventh in the Belgian Grand Prix, Siffert sadly demonstrated that his new Lotus, the 49B, was badly needed when once again, as Jackie Stewart won the race in the wet, his gearbox let him down on the sixtieth out of the 90 laps.

Faithful to his maxim — his only one — that he must run in as many races as possible, Seppi did a deal with the Hart-Ski Organization who had founded a small team with two Porsches 910 as their mounts. So, on any of his free Sundays, in company with Steinemann and Spoerri, Siffert took part in second-line races in which he would drive like one possessed to get victory in the 2-litre class. The engine capacity didn't matter much; the great thing for Seppi was to be racing, to drive his car to the limits of its capability, whatever that might be.

After Spa and Zandvoort, the French Grand Prix at Rouen was also run in the rain. Although the track was dry at the start, Siffert lost 25 seconds when his starter refused to work. On the second lap he was stopped by a blaze which completely barred his way: forty years old, Jo Schlesser, in his first Formula One race, was burned to death in his Honda. After Clark, Spence and Scarfiotti, he was the fourth victim in three months to this sport at once so sublime and so cruel.

The Lotus 49B with Ford engine was just ready for the British Grand Prix. Rob Walker's mechanics, Tony and Jean-Pierre, had spent the whole week before the race pushing ahead with the final assembly. The finishing details, the driver's seat and the rear-view mirrors, had to be fitted on the spot at Brands Hatch, which meant that Joseph lost the first hour of practice. On the last session the Fribourgeois got fourth best time which put him on the second row of the grid beside Jochen Rindt. Good cheer reigned in the Walker camp; the car suited Seppi extremely well and the new stabilising wing at the back seemed just right.

Rob slept badly the night before the race; violent stomach pains kept him awake, and he was not in very good form when, with his wife Betty, he met Seppi, Sabine and Guy von der Weid just before the start. Taking advantage of the better acceleration, Siffert took Amon's Ferrari as soon as the flag dropped and found himself in third place behind the two works Lotus driven by Jacky Oliver and Graham Hill — who went into the lead on the third lap but had to retire on the twenty-seventh lap with a broken half-shaft. Joseph now lay second, behind Oliver, whose car was losing oil, so much so that Seppi had to slow down to wipe his goggles. Amon seized the opportunity to overtake, tucking himself in between the two Lotus. But Siffert turned on the pressure. On lap 43 of the 80-lap race, he re-took the New Zealander. Another lap and Oliver retired, like Graham a victim of transmission trouble.

For the first time in his life, Joseph Siffert was leading in a Formula One race counting for the Drivers' World Championship, pursued by a works Ferrari. In the pits the tension was terrific. Inwardly very nervous, Rob managed to appear impassive: on each lap he recorded his young driver's time and tried not to look at his stopwatch too often. However, he could not prevent his thoughts running ahead; 'Could we perhaps win the British Grand Prix? Even with Stirling Moss, I never dared to hope for something like that!' he said to himself.

On the track, a tremendous duel was raging: almost as if glued to Siffert's Lotus, Amon attacked relentlessly, watching for a mistake, waiting for a tiny error which he could turn to his advantage. For 30 laps the two men were locked in combat, driving right on the limit of both drivers and the machines.

A few laps from the end, Rob saw Tony his mechanic put out a small churn of petrol. 'Is he going to need that?' he asked anxiously.

'No, I hope not, but you never know,' the mechanic replied.

Then, before the end of the race, the loudspeaker broadcast that this victory would be the first for the Walker team since Stirling Moss had won the German Grand Prix in 1961, and the first for Jo Siffert.

Rob did not approve of the announcement at all; he thought it was a bad omen.

Only three laps to go; Amon began to lose ground a little, his tyres were losing some of their grip. Finally, Jo Siffert won the British Grand Prix in 2 hours 01 minutes 20.3 seconds, at the record average speed of 105 mph; he had also set up a new lap record in 1 minute 29.7 seconds at 106 mph. His triumph was complete. Second, Chris Amon finished four and four tenths of a second behind the Swiss.

In the pits everyone was delirious: Rob burst into a cheer of joy and then became once again the perfect English gentleman — his face tired but creased with a huge grin.

Radiant, Jean-Pierre ran out onto the track to meet Seppi as he finished his lap of honour.

The reception was terrific and Joseph received the congratulations of the Duke of Kent and Earl Mountbatten; then, standing on the rostrum, he was garlanded with flowers before the national anthems were played. Next, the victorious Lotus 49B was, according to custom, mounted on a trailer and towed around the course by a tractor on an official lap of honour. To the television commentator who asked for his impressions, Joseph replied in French, simply: *'C'est la premiere fois!'*

The lap of honour was more than a triumph. No driver had ever been more popular. In the big car park behind the pits thousands of motorists were blowing their horns to show their support and admiration for this young foreign driver, hardly known, who had driven his English car to victory for Rob Walker whose private team had triumphed again after seven years of waiting.

Seppi was beaming. He took in all the honour and goodwill of the crowd – he both valued it and at the same time seemed almost embarrassed by it. 'Of all my dreams, the best one was always that I had won the British Grand Prix in the home of motor racing,' he told Betty Walker, who was so happy that she was almost in tears.

Escorted by Rob, Guy, Georges Blanc and a crowd of fans, Seppi went to the circuit restaurant. On the way he suddenly found himself face to face with Jean Tinguely, sitting on the grass, waiting happily. The two men looked at each other without speaking; the sculptor did not get up. The looks they exchanged were more explicit than any speech. There was no need for Joseph and Jean to talk; they were both on the crest of a wave and their unspoken pleasure was too strong for words. After gulping down his champagne, Seppi turned to Guy who had been working for some time in London: 'Could you take me to the airport?'

'You can't do that,' replied Guy. 'You know there is a party at Graham Hill's house tonight, and tomorrow is the drivers' cricket match. You must observe the traditions!'

'No. I promised the Germans that I would race tomorrow at Hockenheim, and I don't want to disappoint them. For me everything must go on, and above all, the racing.'

A few moments to collect his luggage and to say goodbye, and Seppi climbed into Guy's little Cooper with the Fribourg number plates, destination Heathrow. Sabine would return on the Monday with Georges and Josianne.

'Just think what it was like,' Guy von der Weid told me later, 'to drive across London with beside me the chap who had just won the British Grand Prix. I don't think I have ever driven so badly!'

At Fribourg the news of Seppi's victory had hit the town with the force of an explosion and he again was worthily celebrated. 'Is it true that everyone was drunk?' Rob Walker asked me one day.

That evening, with a few friends, I decided to go and call on Seppi's mother and congratulate her, at Granges-Paccot. We knocked on the door and found her all alone, sitting in the half-light, waiting for some more television screening, with before her a little table on which were two candles and a litre of red wine and a glass. Overcome, Mamma Siffert hadn't yet really taken in her son's achievement: she talked about him a lot, recalling many memories of his childhood. Banal really, I longed to know the answer to one question, and in the end I put it to her: 'Are you ever afraid,' I asked.

'Of course, I am always afraid, but I have confidence: and if not I, his mother, who else could believe in him?'

At Hockenheim Siffert did not actually race. He had not done any practice and the Porsche 910 was not properly prepared. All he did was a lap of honour before the race. In the afternoon he telephoned Fribourg and told me that he would arrive that evening and would go the Rex. The

130

tearoom was jampacked when he arrived, to a tremendous ovation. Nervous, he turned to me: 'Let's have a quick drink and then we must go off to my mother's place — there are too many people here.'

Mamma Siffert, whom Seppi had telephoned as he went through Basle, had prepared roesti with ham and dripping, one of the dishes her son was particularly fond of — and she welcomed him home with some emotion. Then, in the company of his friends, Seppi recounted, with a wealth of detail and gesture, the whole story of his victorious race. The rejoicings of the Siffert family were rather spoiled on the Monday morning by the arrival of bad news: on the way back, Georges's Cadillac had been badly damaged in a collision. Sabine had been quite seriously hurt, though luckily she was not in any danger.

The next Sunday Siffert was in Italy where, together with Rico Steinemann, he was going to try and show that he could go faster in the Hart-Ski Porsche 910 than the works Alfa-Romeo 33s. Running through the Appennines, the circuit was 62 kilometres long and terribly twisty.

The first time round, Seppi was 4 seconds ahead of the leading Alfa; on the second lap, he had turned in a new lap record of 31 minutes 21 seconds and he had increased his lead to 30 seconds.

The second car was 1 minute 43 seconds behind when Steinemann took over, but his team-mate was not on form; too nervous, he spun three times and had a minor shunt. The car was 5 minutes 30 seconds behind the Bianchi/Vaccarella Alfa when Seppi took over again. Seppi drove like a fury but the gap was too big for him to close. The Siffert/Steinemann partnership finished the race two minutes behind the winners. Beside himself, Joseph did not mince his words in ticking Rico off — who however had just received an offer from the Porsche works to be their team manager for 1969.

Two days later the Siffert's temper had improved when, in

Fribourg, the local ACS held a reception in honour of the winner of the British Grand Prix. Graham Hill, Jackie Stewart and Jo Bonnier were there to compliment their rival and friend who had proved that he really belonged to the elite of world championship drivers. Resounding throughout the world of sport in Switzerland, the victory at Brands Hatch had above all impressed the experts, the drivers and those responsible for Formula One; and so it was a Siffert classified among the great who went out to the Nurburgring for the German Grand Prix.

The managers of Team Lotus and the BRM team, Peter Warr and Tim Parnell, recognized the rise of Seppi, the most formidable of the outsiders. With a competitive machine, Siffert was a threat to any of the other drivers. His rivals were directly impressed by his victory — now they knew for sure what they were up against. Admittedly there had been his successes at Enna over Jim Clark, but Graham Hill himself had put these down rather to good luck than talent: 'This last race was something altogether different . . . '

Among the journalists, some of them were not all that surprised. Bernard Cahier wasn't at all. The gentlemen of the Press have plenty of time to discover and appreciate the prowess of future champions. 'Seppi was certainly a bit wild at first, but his achievements with the Lotus-BRM in 1963 and his great courage had convinced me that he was in the top class,' the French writer told me.

Widely recognised now, Siffert's courage and perseverance were undisputed. And in addition his kindness and good spirits played a large part in the bond which his admirers felt for him. In Switzerland Siffert rapidly became a kind of legend, criticised when he had to retire, lauded to the skies when he won, but in any case always talked about.

Everything went wrong with the German Grand Prix, beginning with the weather: rain and mist enveloped the Nurburgring. As soon as he got to the circuit, with Bernard

132

Blancpain, he managed to lose control of his car on a corner and went off the track, luckily without doing much harm: 'Call yourself a Formula One driver?' Macado taunted him. The race was a real nightmare; the fog was so dense that one could hardly see. Rob Walker almost felt relieved when his driver stopped on the sixth lap with ignition trouble.

There wasn't much wrong with the next four races and Seppi won the lot. At Hockenheim and at Enna he won with the Porsche 910. Then, as usual, driving his Formula One Lotus-Ford he won the Les Rangiers hill-climb and set up a new absolute record. Joseph did not particularly enjoy hill-climbs which are less interesting and often more danger-ous than a circuit. But this epreuve was unique because it took place in Switzerland, and the Swiss public, his own public, could come without a long and expensive journey, in which any ordinary race would involve them.

The last but one endurance race of the year, the Grand Prix of Austria, was run over a shorter distance this year, over 500 kilometres. So Joseph decided to drive solo without a co-driver in his Porsche 908. The absence of Ford made the race a great deal less interesting and Siffert won without difficulty. Garlanded and applauded, the Fribourgeois sud-denly, right on the rostrum, made a strange gesture — he took off his laurel wreath and hung it over one shoulder. The explanation was simple. There were two badges sewn on his overalls and at least one of them would have to be hidden by the enormous wreath. 'You don't want to kill the goose that lays the golden eggs,' Seppi told me; he knew that the result of the photographer's effort would certainly get published all over the place.

Over 10,000 Swiss set off on the first weekend of September for Monza, in the hope of seeing a new victory for Jo Siffert — and the Fribourg driver would very much have liked not to disappoint them. But he also had a further worry: for some time now, Franco Lini had promised him a reply from the Commendatore Enzo Ferrari about whether or not Siffert would be driving for Maranello in 1969. It was not a simple problem; Seppi was already driving for Porsche and it was going to be very difficult to share his talents between the two rival teams — running on a Sunday in a Formula One car for one, and during the following week in a sports car for the other. Siffert would give priority to Formula One and he would therefore have to leave the German factory if they wanted to run a works single-seater: 'Well,' he would ask Franco Lini every time he met him, 'has the Commendatore decided yet?'

'No, not yet, but any time now,' the journalist would reply, in his capacity as part-time team manager.

For a long time now, Lini had longed to see Siffert drive a Ferrari. It would be quite a serious matter; in losing Seppi Porsche would at a stroke drop thirty or forty per cent of their chances of winning, for there was no other driver in endurance races up to his standard except Jacky Ickx and he was driving a Ford for John Wyer's team.

Inwardly, Seppi was not very put-out by the time things were taking to get settled; he had not really made up his own mind, torn between his practical interests and sentiment. Ferrari would of course provide him with a first-class car, but he felt so at home with Rob Walker that he almost regarded him as a father.

During the race, the Lotus went beautifully and Siffert finished the fifteenth lap leading the pack formation so typical of Monza. But on lap 59 out of 68 laps, a rear shock absorber went, as he was lying in second place behind Denis Hulme, which forced him to retire to the chagrin of his faithful supporters.

For the next race in which the Walker team would compete, a fortnight away, the surroundings were entirely new — it was the Canadian Grand Prix run over the Mont Tremblant circuit. Third in practice, Siffert started for the first time on the front row, but a stone through his radiator forced him to retire by lap 30 — the reverse of what had happened at Brands Hatch when he had hung on to the Ferrari of Chris Amon who had had to retire with transmission trouble, leaving the victory as at Monza to Denny Hulme on the McLaren-Ford. Siffert was slightly consoled when he learned that he had set up a new official lap record with a time of 1 minute 35.1 seconds at an average speed of 100.32 mph, for which he was congratulated by the Prime Minister of Canada himself, Pierre Trudeau.

An unheard-of departure, because of the strike which had paralysed the whole of France in the spring, the Le Mans 24-Hour Race was held in mid-September. Siffert was one of the leading favourites. The town of Le Mans was shrouded in rain as the Fribourgeois set off like a whirlwind hot on the heels of Elford, and for four hours the two Porsches provided a spectacle of rare intensity.

'I just had to follow the white line,' Seppi explained to Bisule later, who wanted to know how one could see driving along at over 180 mph in the rain, following close behind another car.

But after only four hours the transmission went, and the leading Siffert/Herrmann car pulled into the pits for good.

As had become a custom since 1964, Jo Siffert finished in the United States Grand Prix at Watkins Glen. And this year again the Swiss driver clocked up some points for the world championship when he finished sixth in spite of having to make an emergency stop five laps from the end.

When he got back to Europe, he had three races — at Hockenheim where he was accompanied by Georges Blanc and a charming young lady known as Simone, at Rome and at Albi.

The final round in the Drivers' World Championship was on the 3rd November in Mexico. The race looked like being quite something: Graham Hill, Jackie Stewart and Denny

135

Hulme could all still win the title. However, it was Jo Siffert who put in best time in practice – 1 minute 45.22 seconds – ahead of Chris Amon. For the first time the Swiss would start from pole position. The three pretenders for the world title were immediately behind the two heroes of Brands Hatch.

On Sunday morning, Seppi went to Mass. Before the start, Colin Chapman and Peter Warr from Team Lotus had a chat with him and asked him to help Hill on his way to the title. 'For the Lotus factory the World Championship had a special importance in 1968 – the year of Jim Clark's death,' Peter Warr told me much later.

For Seppi, the first aim was to win, and so also was the second. As for the champions, they were big enough to sort the matter out between themselves!

The Swiss fluffed his start and for the first time round he was eighth. Then he really got going and by lap 16 he was in the lead in front of Hill. Hulme had already retired after an excursion off the track. But Joseph did not stop there; he rapidly built up a useful lead on Graham who couldn't believe his eyes at the way Siffert cut the corners, just missing the low safety barriers. Then, suddenly, trouble. A very small trouble, certainly, but one which meant that he had to make a pit stop. The bolt holding the accelerator cable had come out. In three minutes, Tony Cleverley fitted a new one, taken from the spare engine, and Siffert was off once again. What followed was so exciting that the crowd forgot the race for the title. Breaking the lap record continually on each successive lap, he finally did one in 1 minute 44.23 seconds, at an average speed of 107.26 mph – only a second less than the time he had set up in practice. This performance alone was remarkable. Joseph overtook all his rivals, but the race was too short – or the delay too long – to recover all the lost ground, and he finished in sixth place in a race which Rob Walker always maintained was the most fantastic of his career. 'Thirty laps more and I would have won,' Seppi told me when he got back.

That evening, as Rob and Seppi settled down to celebrate what they felt they could justifiably call a success, Franco Lini tried to get in touch with Enzo Ferrari.

'Well, anything doing?' Siffert asked him during the evening.

'No, but it may still turn up,' replied the journalist.

'It's too late. I can't wait any longer: I'm doing a deal with Rob and Porsche.'

Rob Walker was delighted. After four years together Seppi had been very near leaving. BRM had already suggested that they would withdraw their offer to Seppi if Walker wanted to keep him. 'Talk to him — he must decide,' said Rob to Tim Parnell. Walker wanted very much to keep Seppi but he would not bind him. It would not have been fair to tie him up if he could run a better car, he thought.

Jo Siffert was doubly rewarded for his brilliant 1968 season — the BP Trophy was awarded to him again and also the President's Cup of the ACS. His business affairs prospered and Jo had just acquired a garage right in the middle of Fribourg, but on the private side things were not so good. After living happily together for some years, during which he and Sabine had done very well for each other, they had drifted apart and were now separated. On his side, Seppi had been in love for some time now with Simone — a girl from Fribourg who worked as a medical secretary in Geneva.

The weeks that he had to spend in the Argentine would give him time in between the four races of the Temporada Series, for which he would drive a Formula Two car, to rest and to do some thinking. In spite of BMW pulling out of racing, Siffert was given a drive by the Pederzani Brothers on a Tecno. His colleague in the team would be another Swiss, Clay Regazzoni, who came from the Tessin. Very small, the car was good; the front was literally glued to the road whilst

137

the back end had a tendency to slide, which meant that the driver had to adjust accordingly. As for its sense of direction, it was so hard to keep it going forward in a straight line that Seppi's hands were bleeding after the first practice.

From Buenos Aires, Siffert went by car with the Swiss journalist Adrianno Cimarosti to Cordova and then three hundred miles on to San Juan over the desert. He took a little time off to laugh and enjoy himself. The evening before one race there was a dance in the hotel garden, and the noise was so infernal that the driver just could not sleep. Finally, he got up and fairly set the place humming.

Although half on holiday, he did not forget his business affairs. Two or three times a week he would telephone to Fribourg and if he saw any second-hand car dealers he would hurry in. This was how he came to buy, for 450 dollars, a 1921 Model T Ford in perfect going order. The transport back to Switzerland looked like being expensive. However, with a bit of help from Juan Manuel Fangio he managed to pass it off as a car which had been competing in the Temporada Series and so its journey was free of charge!

He finished the 1968 season on the 22nd December at Buenos Aires with a third place behind the invincible V6 Dino Ferraris. The final score was not bad: Joseph, with twelve points, was seventh in the list of the drivers of the world.

CHAPTER SEVEN

With the object of giving the Formula One constructors a bit more time between seasons, the South African Grand Prix was put off until the first weekend in March. So for Jo Siffert the first race of the season was the Daytona Beach 24-Hour Race at the beginning of February, in which he would race with Hans Herrmann for the last time. The undisputed top driver for the Stuttgart firm, Siffert did not undervalue the experience and great qualities of his co-driver, but Herrmann did not go fast enough: the Ferrari come-back presented a serious threat to Porsche and endurance races were going to attract as much attention as Grands Prix. Rico Steinemann, the sporting director of the German Marque, had definitely signed up Brian Redman, who had been Jacky Ickx's co-driver in the John Wyer team. For the first race of the season the British driver would share a car with Vic Elford.

Porsche was fielding a whole regiment: five cars, ten drivers, thirty-five mechanics — the team seemed to be invincible, so much so that Steinemann did not lay down any tactics at the briefing before the race; he just gave them a few general running instructions and told each driver to go at his own pace. Bernard Blancpain who came along, was amazed: he had been expecting a real council of war!

Siffert dominated the race from the start but after an hour he suddenly pulled into the pits: red and grimy, he leapt out of the car and told Bott, one of the Porsche engineers, what the trouble was, the dust and sand had completely blocked up the air intake which ventilated the cockpit. Siffert, who was driving in helmet and sun goggles, simply could not breathe as he ran onto the celebrated banking of Daytona and was driving at over 185 mph. He managed to knock out the filter element as he drove and all the muck flew back in his face! Luckily, he was more frightened than hurt and repairs did not take very long.

Then, one by one, the Porsche drivers were overcome by fumes from faulty exhaust pipes; Mitter and Elford were so bad that they had to be taken to hospital.

Herrmann was seventh when he took over the wheel, and for the next ten hours the two men made a fantastic come-back; by the early hours of the morning they had climbed back into second place. At this moment fate struck again. One after the other, the five Porsches retired, this time for good, with broken camshaft gears. Made of a new alloy, they just did not last. Porsche had to face up to a major defeat.

Seppi did not have much time to fuss about it: he had to catch the next plane to Europe. There wasn't much time. Driving at over 100 mph along the American roads, Macado and Kurt Ahrens searched the sky for police helicopters so that the law could not overtake them.

A month later he took fourth place in the South African Grand Prix with his Lotus-Ford and three points in the Drivers' World Championship. At the prize-giving he met one of the McLaren mechanics, Eddy Wyss from Zurich. The only two Swiss who were really participating in the Formula One circus, they soon became good friends.

After a short stay in Fribourg, Seppi set off for Florida. Not wanting another debacle like Daytona, Porsche had organized a real practice session at Sebring, where they were going to compete later in the 12-Hour Race. The new 3-litre Spiders were thoroughly tested out and were in such good nick that Joseph knocked six seconds off the record recently set up by Mike Spence. During the private practice, Seppi did not show himself up as a great test driver — perhaps because he was so used to driving mediocre cars. Making up for their shortcomings by his masterly driving, he always said that the car was going fine! On top of this the difficulty he had in expressing himself in words and a tendency to concentrate too much on the engine, at the expense of the rest of the car, was not a great help to the engineers. And then, really, Seppi loathed practice sessions during which he would sometimes have to wait hours until the car was ready. He hated hanging about. The other drivers, who were better at test running, could really get the car 90 per cent correctly set up; then at that stage, Siffert, who could drive that much faster, would go into collaboration with Flegel, one of the Porsche mechanics, to work out the finishing touches.

Equipped for the first and the last time with two stabilising wings, one in the front and one at the back, the Lotus once again took fourth place in the Race of Champions at Brands Hatch. But the race did not count for the World Championship.

Porsches' hopes were dashed again in the Sebring 12-Hour Race: suspension trouble forced Siffert and Redman to retire and victory went to Ickx and Oliver on the Ford GT40.

The Swiss driver had to get back home again quickly; on the Tuesday his new garage, in the middle of Fribourg, was going to be officially opened. Having secured the Porsche and Alfa-Romeo agencies, he had laid on a big reception, and among the 500 invited guests were Rob Walker and Rico Steinemann. After a tour round the premises, the BBC film of the British Grand Prix was shown in a nearby cinema. Sitting beside Seppi, I heard him relive the last moments of his victorious race: 'Careful, only three more laps, it's not the moment to make a mistake — Amon is there, waiting for just that.'

The reminiscences of Brands Hatch went on long after the film was over: in the small hours, with a few close friends, we found ourselves in the garage shop where Seppi, gloved and helmeted, sitting in a bucket seat, won once again the British Grand Prix — 'just doing a few laps of the circuit.' In cracking form, Rob Walker produced a stirring imitation of the noise made by the Lotus-Ford which produced a few indignant telephone calls from the owners of the first-floor premises above . . .

The reliving of this victory seemed to be a good omen — three weeks later Jo Siffert and Brian Redman gave Porsche their first win for some time when they won the 500-mile race at Brands Hatch. Prospects before the race had not seemed particularly good: on the line, with ten minutes to go, the mechanics were still working on the Porsche 908 of which the ignition was hardly working at all. Finally, Seppi started some 20 bhp down on the other Porsche drivers. However, Siffert's skill and his good teamwork with Brian Redman made up for this. The characters of the two men harmonised well. Both were calm and cool, not given to a great deal of talking; each respected the other. Redman was not perhaps quite as determined to win as Siffert, but his job was above all to keep the car out in front or in whatever position Seppi had got it. Brian did this to perfection and could always be relied on to increase the pace if this should be necessary. Well balanced in every respect, the Siffert/Redman partnership had a good chance of keeping in front throughout the season.

Ten days later, Friday the 25th April, they confirmed what the Press had forecast for them by winning the Monza 1000-Kilometre Race. But the opposition was also there: the first time round two 312 Ferraris led the race, followed by the Siffert Porsche which soon afterwards slipped in between the red cars of Rodriguez and Andretti. Third time round, to the dismay of the Italian supporters, the Swiss went into the lead, and never gave it up again except for a few moments due to the breathing troubles which are peculiar to Monza.

Two days later, BMW's efforts began to bear fruit when Seppi came in second behind Stewart in the Eifelrennen run over the Nurburgring.

Joseph had really got the wind behind him now. In Spain he tried to persuade Rob to fit up the Lotus with enormous wings like those on the cars of Graham Hill and Jochen Rindt. 'I will fit them as soon as I am sure that they are strong enough,' Rob told a disappointed Seppi in the taxi taking them to the Montjuich circuit at Barcelona. 'But for the time being you'll just have to make do with the small wings.'

Once again Walker was proved right; one after the other, at the same point, Hill and Rindt had fearful crashes after their wings had packed up. Graham was unscathed, but Jochen had to be taken to hospital. Both of them had been incredibly luckly. Lying second behind Amon, Seppi retired — after running a third of the distance — with oil pump trouble, and the victory went to Jackie Stewart. But Siffert was not too put out: Ron Tauranac, the chief designer at Brabhams, had made a definite approach; he was preparing two machines for Indianapolis and would like the Swiss to drive one in the famous 500-mile race which would take place in a few months' time. However, Siffert was a little too greedy over the starting money; Jack Brabham called off negotiations and Peter Revson was given the second car.

The 4½-litre Porsche 917 made its first appearance the following weekend for the 1000-Kilometre race over the tremendously fast circuit at Spa-Francorchamps not far from Liege. Siffert practised hard on the new monster, of which the living quarters were so far forward that the pedals were actually ahead of the front axle, but the car did not seem quite right and he decided to start the race in the old hack 908 on which all the drivers had been having a go. In spite of

the long distance, the race ran with all the excitement of a
Grand Prix. Undisputed experts on fast circuits with long
bends, Jo Siffert and Pedro Rodriguez put on a fantastic
show at speeds of almost 150 mph. The Ferrari followed the
Porsche like a shadow in spite of problems overtaking slower
cars.

Suddenly, in the left and right of Eau Rouge Siffert found
himself behind the much slower Porsche 907 of von Wendt
and overtook him on the inside of the bend. Behind him,
coming out of the S, Rodriguez had no choice: if he braked
he would lose his tow from the Porsche. So he pushed
through, but in doing so he touched the German drivers'
car — which flew off the track, went through an advertising
hoarding and finished up in a hazel thicket. Fortunately
unhurt, he complained to Seppi when Redman had taken
over the wheel about Rodriguez's behaviour. But the Swiss
was unsympathetic.

Siffert was not too fond of some of the slower cars which
seemed to him more like mobile chicanes; their drivers were
usually less experienced, and were often so absorbed in their
driving that they sometimes forgot all about the faster cars
which were duelling over their heads. And when Siffert and
Rodriguez were at each other's throats it was certainly a
battle royal!

The Grand Prix of Monaco did not get off to a very good
start; in the first practice session, although he had already
broken the lap record twice, Siffert braked too hard for the
Gasworks Corner and went into the straw bales, breaking the
nose of his Lotus. That evening, as a result of the accidents of
Hill and Rindt at Barcelona, the Commission Sportive
Internationale announced a ban, with immediate effect, on
stabilising wings fixed directly to the rear suspension; from
now on the wings would have to be fitted to the actual
engine block. The next day, after only three laps of practice,
the engine blew up at Ste Devote at the foot of the Casino

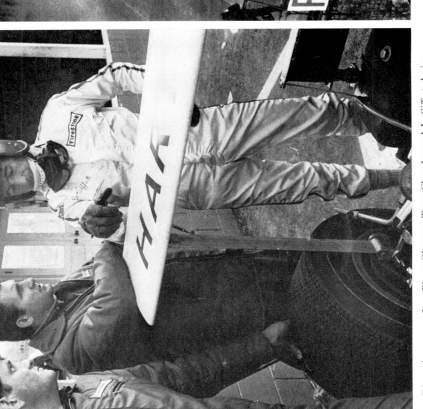

The will to win: Siffert, left, and Rodriguez, right, storm through the S, door-handle to doorhandle, at Spa in the 1970 1000-kilometre race

Discussion group: Jean-Pierre Oberson, Tony Cleverley and Jo Siffert during practice for the United States Grand Prix, 1968

Driving partnership: Jo Siffert and
Brian Redman

Literary partnership: Jacques Deschenaux
Jo Siffert

Can-Am 1971—the exploits of the small Porsche amazed the Americans

hill. Rob had only one spare engine, the one from the 1968 Brands Hatch car which the mechanics worked through most of the night to install. During last practice on Saturday, Seppi managed to turn fifth best time which put him on the third row of the grid beside John Surtees. But the engine was not delivering its full power; after 8000 revs it just ran out of steam.

Plugs, electrics, fuel connections, everything was taken down, checked and changed during the night before the race. At six o'clock in the morning, Tony Cleverley even tried it out on the track, waking up the Monegasasques a little early, but there was nothing doing, the Lotus just would not run any better.

Right from the start of the race it seemed as if the engine was only running on seven cylinders, and Siffert did not seem to have much chance of finishing the race. But Seppi made up for the lack of power by the skill of his driving. As he stormed down the hill into Mirabeau, everyone in the Casino stands would rise to their feet to get a better view — they just couldn't believe that he would get out of the corner without hitting the barriers. In the end, after both Stewart and Amon had retired, Siffert finished the Monaco Grand Prix in third place only 35 seconds behind Graham Hill, the winner, and 17 behind Piers Courage's Brabham.

It was only after they had stripped the engine right down that they discovered the cause of the trouble: the camshaft was broken at one end, putting one of the two valves for the last cylinder completely out of action!

A new victory in the 1000-Kilometre race at Nurburgring was enough for Porsche to win their first Sports Car Constructors' World Championship. The Stuttgart factory had all the aces in their hands, running six 908s; all except one that is — Ferrari had entered a 312P Spider to be driven by two formidable operators: Pedro Rodriguez and Chris Amon.

Practice started with a drama; coming unstuck as it went over a bump, Siffert's car literally took off, turned right over and thumped back onto the track, trapping its driver. Well strapped in, Siffert was unhurt but at any moment a blaze could be started — and help seemed a long time coming. Finally, some officials arrived who were reassured to hear Seppi swearing away and yelling at them to get him out of his unpleasant predicament! 'I had the worst fright of my life,' he told me when I arrived at the circuit the next day.

The car was certainly not going to be any use, and Siffert had two alternatives; one was the hack car, the other was a 908 entered by Porsche Austria. Seppi tried them both in practice, but he made the best time on the hack, lapping the 14-mile circuit in 8 minutes 0.2 seconds. Rico Steinemann, however, advised him to run the other car, which although less well prepared, was a good deal newer. Piech, who was after all an engineer, didn't think that either of them were much good! Seppi wanted above all a good engine for he could perform prodigies of driving with a less good chassis, but he could not extract more power than the engine could produce. It was up to him to choose. The Porsche team might be German, but it was not regimented — or at least not as far as Siffert was concerned. In the end, it was the driver who took the risk and so he made the decisions.

Joseph opted for Rico's solution; during practice on the Friday he stopped at the pits and told the team manager: 'This car isn't at all stable; it took off again, but this time luckily it landed the right way up!'

Rico did not doubt for a moment that this was the truth: the two exhausts and the jacking points were all badly bent. An aerodynamics problem was going to have to be rapidly resolved.

In the Porsche camp, the drivers all had different views: the Germans thought that Seppi's enthusiasm had been a bit damped down by the accident, and that their chances of winning were almost certain. Brian Redman, for his part, was very nervous. He had no doubts on Siffert's account, but on his own: he was not familiar with the circuit and its 170 corners, and he only turned in a very so-so time. Brian didn't want to lose the race for Seppi, particularly as the second best time, only a tenth of a second down on the Swiss, had been put up by the Ferrari; he asked Steinemann if he could replace him with a driver more at home on that circuit.

Rico suggested that Gerhard Mitter might share with Siffert but the German driver refused: if they won, all the credit would go to Siffert whereas, without the support of Redman, the Swiss might be beaten by the Mitter/Schultz partnerhsip entirely German — who would then have the double honour of winning the race and beating Siffert, the undisputed master of sports-racing cars. The affair soon got worked up and the sensational German Press gave it prominent space on the Saturday.

But Seppi just laughed about it. His first worry was to restore the confidence of his co-driver. After asking him to be as tough with himself as he could, he took him round, out of practice, in his own private Porsche; they drove round for two laps whilst Siffert explained to him the secrets of the Nurburgring.

After the start, Indianpolis-style, Siffert and Amon soon saw Mitter and Stommelen tuck themselves between them and then nip past. But the first time round the Swiss was already in the lead, followed by Mitter and Amon, who took over second place. Siffert led as if on rails. On the third lap, as he was already beginning to overtake the back markers, a slow car which had not seen him moved over and hit him just as he was going past, catching the front edge of the Porsche's stabilising wing. The car could continue, but the roadholding was affected. However, this didn't prevent Redman from putting in a first-class stint at the wheel and giving his partner the luxury of an increased lead.

A little after the halfway mark, the Ferrari went out with clutch trouble and some problem over tyres. Amon had, however, put in fastest lap. The front car steadily increased its lead. After 900 kilometres the lead was so commanding that, with two laps left to go, Seppi asked Rico, as a special favour, if he would stop Brian and let him take over: 'I would just love to cross the finishing line myself. Up till now Brian's always finished the race!' Siffert told Steinemann, a bit like a spoilt child.

Steinemann hesitated a moment and then agreed; the only real risk was if the engine failed to re-start, but Seppi took the responsibility and everything went off perfectly: the Siffert/Redman partnership won their fourth victory of the season and gave Porsche their first World Championship title. The German triumph was complete: the six Porsches took the first six places.

Decked out in their gilded laurel wreaths, Siffert and Redman flanked Steinemann for a photograph. Then Seppi took his off and hung it round Rico's neck; Brian did the same with his. The team manager was deeply touched but Seppi had the last laugh: 'It is just moments like this when you have to think of your publicity contract,' he told me, 'you can't see anything through those laurel leaves!'

That evening, at the prizegiving, Siffert personally insisted that the organizers should give the ring, always awarded to winners at the Nurburgring, to his co-driver. Had he not put in the second best time of all the Porsche 908s which competed? On that day, Brian had proved something — perhaps as much to himself as to the other drivers. The Press gave a lot of space to Porsche's victory. From Italy, Franco Lini wrote that Siffert had been the key man in the championship; he alone had gone faster than the Ferrari 312 and if he had transferred to Maranello, then the title also would have fetched up in a different camp.

After this new victory, only three endurance races still did not feature in Jo Siffert's score card; the Targa Florio in which Seppi had not been able to compete this year because it was held on the same day at the Spanish Grand Prix; the 6-Hour Race at Watkins Glen, and the Le Mans 24-Hour Race which would be held on the Sarthe circuit in a fortnight's time.

Siffert was determined to win this race which, if it was not the most interesting, was certainly — with Indianapolis — the most popular throughout the world. He decided not to drive the new Porsche 917, faster but somehow not as well set up as the 908 Spider which had already earned him numerous successes.

For a change, because of the French elections, the race was started at 2 o'clock in the afternoon. Siffert went across the track at a hell of a pace and leapt into his car with such vigour that he almost went in head first. The first time round he was third behind the two 917s of Stommelen and Elford which were much quicker down the Mulsanne straight but which, as he had foreseen, would soon have to make regular pit stops for adjustments. So without having to force the engine or his skill, Siffert rapidly went to the head of the race. 'I am trying to nurse my engine as much as possible,' he told me as Redman took over. 'Down les Hunaudieres I am not going over 300 kilometres an hour which means I can have a look at the television helicopter.'

Redman handed the wheel over, still in the lead. Seppi set out again, but not for long; a few laps later he stopped and then he had to retire for an idiotic reason — the streamlining of the 908 was not allowing enough cooling in the back of the car and an oil pipe had burst. As a result, the oil in the gearbox had become so hot that it was impossible to change gear. Seppi was disgusted. He left his car, like a dead bull, and sat for a long time in the pits with his head in his hands.

The next day he took the road for Vichy, where Simone was waiting for him; in fact she was not only waiting for

149

Seppi but also for her child which was almost due . . . On the road he heard the exciting end of the 24-Hours on the wireless: Ickx and Herrmann were elbow to elbow on the last lap. 'Ickx will win,' he said briefly. When I expressed surprise, he went on: 'It's at just such a moment that one sees the real difference between a Grand Prix driver and a sports car driver.'

Ickx won on the old Ford GT40, ahead of the German driver's Porsche. Seppi produced a little bottle of whisky and we drank to the Belgian driver's health. 'You see, if I don't win, Porsche doesn't win either,' he told me with a wink. 'That's a very good argument for when I have to sign a new contract!'

Then after a couple of days in Vichy, we went on to Switzerland — Seppi correcting the faults of the wretched driver that I am, compared to him. 'Make mistakes like that, and you'll wake up dead one morning,' he told me with a grin, as I put the car dangerously sideways going into a bend.

His pleasure over the second place he carried off with his Lotus-Ford in the Dutch Grand Prix, behind Jackie Stewart, after a relentless duel with Graham Hill, was somewhat dampened when he learned that I had very seriously damaged his Porsche going off the road. This rather ignominious episode earned me an infernal rocket that even the army could not have matched.

After retiring again at Reims with the Formula Two BMW, we took the road for Clermont-Ferrand where the French Grand Prix would take place. But the Grand Prix rather took second place when, on the evening of the first practice, at Vichy, Simone gave birth to a small daughter who was to be called Veronique.

Her father's pleasure was immense. Seppi loved children and up till now he had had to make do with his nephews and nieces.

Having got the world title, the Porsche works did not think

150

it necessary to send a team to America for the next endurance race — the 6-Hour race at Watkins Glen, which would be run the next weekend. All the same, Siffert and Redman found themselves driving a 908 Spider entered by Porsche Austria, and after an almost fratricidal battle with the drivers of the second car in the team, Elford and Attwood, the star team of the sports car world championship constructors won their fifth victory of the season. But the next day Seppi and Brian were for once competing against each other, both at the wheel of identical 908s in a Can-Am Series race over the same circuit. Siffert hadn't got a chance against the 7- and 8-litre monsters developing infinitely more power and he only came in sixth. But it was also in effect a test: Richie Ginther, the former racing driver, who was now the Director of Porsche California, had decided to enter one car in each of the eight remaining races of the Can-Am Series. The object of the exercise was not so much to win — which was really not on in the face of the unbeatable McLaren Chevrolets, but to try and classify as high as possible. To do this, the factory was proposing to turn out a Spider version of the Porsche 917 whose robust engine ought certainly to get the car over the finish line of all the races.

There was not much argument about the choice of driver: knowing the car extremely well from having driven it in numerous private practices at Hockenheim, Jo Siffert was the first pick ahead of any of the American drivers. For Seppi the arrangement was a real blessing. With the Constructors' Championship over, it looked as if he would only be able to race on one or two more Sundays when there was a Formula One Race.

The atmosphere around the British Grand Prix, which took place the following weekend at Silverstone, was quite different to that at Brands Hatch the year before. Siffert was in a bad mood; he just could not get the suspension of the Lotus-Ford set up right, and the car did not hold the road at all well. On top of that, the organizers had forbidden all advertising on the car; Seppi was just on the point of going back to Switzerland. Finally, taking into account his favourable position on the world championship table, he did agree to start.

On the morning of the race he was out for a short practice run on one of the old runways of the wartime aerodrome at Silverstone. Reaching over 150 mph at the end of one run, Seppi tried to brake but all that happened was a couple of showers of sparks: a mechanic had forgotten to fit the brake pads. Spinning and swerving, the driver just managed to avoid disaster, but it had been a very near thing! In the race, Siffert fought like a tiger in the tight pack made up of Hill, Rodriguez and Courage, but his badly set-up car necessitated a real virtuoso performance in driving. And then, three laps from the end, a breakdown: the mechanics had either miscalculated the petrol consumption or they had perhaps used the same amount as the works Lotus, because Rindt and Hill both suffered from the same misfortune.

It was too much: Seppi was beside himself. After the race, which he had finally finished in eight place, we were all in the truck where he gave the mechanics a dressing-down they would never forget. Rob, from his own point of view, was Rob Walker, looking at it from his own point of view, was also very upset. Suddenly, having told them everything that he had on his mind, Seppi turned to me and said, as if to excuse his fury: 'If anything happens after all, it's me who fetches up in the cemetery, not them!'

All this was soon forgotten, however; Graham Hill's party that evening was a tremendous success and Seppi laughed so much that he had stomach-aches for two days afterwards.

For the first time for ages, Jo had no race booked for the Sunday which followed, so he took advantage of this to go to Vichy for the christening of his daughter Veronique.

Rico Steinemann, however, telephoned him the evening

before he left, and asked him to come straight up to Hockenheim to try out the Can-Am Porsche 917.

'I can't,' replied the driver, 'I am engaged.'

'You can't be; I know you're not racing this weekend.'

'That doesn't matter — I'm still engaged.'

'You are not going to make me believe that you are chasing after a girl!' said Rico, who did not know at all what was going on.

Rob and Seppi had a long discussion when they arrived at the Nurburgring the following Thursday; they had to take some decision. The driver detailed everything that was not to his liking and finally asked for complete control of the car at the factory. Bob agreed to this; the arrangement suited him quite well. With Seppi one talked things over, and then one forgot about them. The episode at Silverstone was already simply an unhappy recollection.

Siffert made a very good start and put himself right on the tail of Jackie Stewart's Matra-Ford — Stewart was already set to be World Champion for 1969. Ickx on the Brabham made a splendid comeback through the field and took the lead at the halfway mark. On the last lap but one, Joseph did not come round. The waiting was agonising; in the pits his mother tried to hide her nervousness. Finally, as he went past, McLaren, who had been one minute behind the Swiss, made a signal to signify that the driver was unhurt. In fact, Seppi had gone off the track after his back suspension had broken. He was more frightened than anything else, but this time again it had been a very near thing. Only four drivers completed the course and so Siffert was credited with fifth place, taking two extra points for World Championship.

Jo Siffert finally agreed to drive the Porsche 917 for the last long-distance race of the season — the Austrian Grand Prix held at Zeltweg. Brian Redman was still worried about the monster, and he asked, as he had at the Nurburgring, not to drive with the Swiss because he was afraid of making him

153

lose the race. Brian lacked confidence in the car. In fact, if the 917 was not a good car in an accident, it was, on the other hand, very much more likely to avoid one — its roadholding was prodigious.

This time the Englishman was allowed to stand down and Siffert won his sixth victory of the season, his first on the Porsche 917, with Kurt Ahrens as co-driver.

Seppi's popularity was now enormous; his fan-mail bore witness to this. Every day he got dozens of letters, mostly from the German-speaking Swiss from Germany, from Austria and from Italy, asking for his autograph, for his advice, or wanting to meet him. Some of them were from passionate admirers, while others sought the magic password to become racing drivers themselves.

One day an extremely long letter arrived at the garage. The Reverend Mother of a Swiss convent asked him to take out an insurance policy to get him to Heaven. The convent was in a dreadful state and the whole building badly needed repairs. She asked the driver to make her a gift of a million francs. And then, she assured him, the Good God would receive him in Heaven, just as soon as he was dead. For several weeks, I kept the letter in a pocket not quite having the courage to show it to its addressee. One day, when Seppi was particularly relaxed, I handed it over to him: as he read through it I noticed that he changed colour; then he put it in his pocket with a grunt. Just as I had, he kept it there for a long time. One evening, at a dinner organized for the benefit of some good work, he found himself sitting beside a distinguished ecclesiastic and so he opened the conversation: 'You know, I don't have to practise my religion any more,' he told him, 'I have an insurance!' — and he handed over the letter. It was the prelate's turn to change colour . . . .

If some of these petitions left him completely unmoved, he did not turn his back on poverty. Seppi had not forgotten his own childhood and the sight of a poor child always touched him. He was particularly generous when it was a question of helping children with damage to the brain. Seppi loved all children too much not to do something about them if he saw them in pain.

The first time out with the Porsche 917A Spider was a success: Siffert took fourth place at Lexington, Ohio, behind the invincible McLaren-Chevrolets of Bruce McLaren and Denny Hulme, and the Ferrari 612P driven by Chris Amon; The Swiss found himself eighth in the general Can-Am classification with sixteen points.

Back in Europe, he just had time to run the BMW in the Formula Two Mediterranean Grand Prix and then Joseph flew out to America again to Elkhart Lake in Wisconsin where the race went less happily: on the seventh lap, running in fourth gear, Seppi intended to change up, but the gear selector slipped and he engaged third gear at over 125 mph. The engine was not in favour of this and blew up; Siffert had to retire.

The next weekend the whole staff of Jo Siffert Automobiles set off for Monza to watch the boss on the job — he had invited all of them to the Italian Grand Prix. But by mid-race one of the pistons was playing up and he had to drop behind the leading pack and finished in eighth place.

Three days later, Siffert flew off for a trip to the United States and Japan, lasting two months. The jaunt started with a success when he came in third in a Can-Am race at Bridgehampton near New York, behind Hulme and McLaren.

The Canadian Grand Prix was held this year at Mosport; during practice, Seppi hit a safety barrier in the bend just before the pits, breaking the front left suspension of his Lotus-Ford which was now getting a bit tired. In the race, a universal joint broke on the fortieth of the ninety laps, when the Swiss was at close quarters with Graham Hill and Jean-Pierre Beltoise, fighting over sixth place.

He did better in the next Can-Am race at Irish Hills in

Michigan, where he drove his Porsche into fourth place, gaining a further 10 points in the general classification, in which he was now fifth. Jo Siffert's popularity was growing in America: the public liked the little Porsche America team which was now almost rivalling the McLarens and Chaparrals with their big Chevrolet engines developing 100 bhp more than the 917.

For Seppi, the United States Grand Prix did not last very long; fifth in practice, the Swiss driver had to retire on the third lap — the race was over 108 laps — after the fuel-injection system broke down. And while Jochen Rindt won his first victory in the Drivers' World Championship, Graham Hill, the reigning world champion, fell victim to a serious accident during the race — though his life was not in danger. The three Lotus entered in the race therefore came out of it with very different results. And Jo's car was certainly beginning to feel its age more and more.

Seppi reviewed the situation but he was not too much worried: Lotus, BRM and Ferrari had already made him offers for the next season. Rob Walker was anxious not to influence him, but he also had made it clear that he did not want to show him the door, in fact very much to the contrary! Then Porsche, through Rico Steinemann, took on

Then Porsche, acting through Rico Steinemann, took on the role of eminence grise; the last thing they wanted was to lose their best sports car driver. The Stuttgart factory would give financial backing to an offer from any team not competing in the Sports Car Manufacturers' World Championship. As for Siffert himself, he wanted above all a good Formula One car — and on that basis alone he would decide whose colours he would carry in the endurance races.

The journey that he was starting the next week would give Seppi time to consider the offers made to him: from New York he was going on to Tokyo and then to Mount Fuji where on the Friday he would race in the Japanese Grand

Prix at the wheel of a Porsche 917 which he was sharing with David Piper.

Practice took place in the early morning in the fog and the Porsche — which apart from Motschenbacher's similar car was the only non-Japanese car competing — could not be tested and run at its proper speed, which made the choice of tyre compound particularly difficult. For Nissan and Datsun who ran regularly on this track at the foot of Fujiyama, the problems had been resolved long before.

Siffert nevertheless went into the lead at the beginning of the race, but after ten laps the poor preparation and the unsuitable tyre compounds obliged him to give up the lead to a Datsun. Hardly had the Japanese driver overtaken him, than the Porsche was showered with oil, to such an extent that they had to make a pit stop to clean the screen. Siffert was soon off again, but this time in the wake of a Nissan and the same thing happened again. A further pit stop. An odd coincidence, Motschenbacher had to stop for exactly the same reason. Thus relegated to a respectful distance from the leaders, the two Porsches were not too worried about the result, but the tyres, tested under foggy conditions, did not adapt themselves to the state of the track and the Siffert/ Piper partnership had four blow-outs and could do no better than a sixth place.

A Red Cross helicopter took Siffert straight to Tokyo where his aeroplane left at 10 o'clock. Thanks to the difference in times, Joseph made up 14 hours and arrived in California 3 hours earlier on the same evening!

Time was precious: the following day was the practice for the next Can-Am race at Laguna Seca. On the warming-up lap before the start of the race, he had a disagreeable experience and found himself being squeezed between the safety barrier and Gurney's McLaren which had pushed out of line; his two stabilising wings were twisted and the Swiss could not start until a lap behind the other 35 contenders. However, he staged a tremendous comeback and after a number of retirements he managed to finish the race in fifth place.

The last race in the Drivers' World Championship, the Mexican Grand Prix, looked like being even more emotive than usual: not only because of the race itself but even more because of the important moves which would be discussed there.

If most of the other drivers were fixed up for 1970, several of the works team had made an offer to Jo Siffert.

Lotus, who had by now contracted Mario Andretti, were ruled out from the start: the directors of the Norwich factory could not agree to a driver dispersing his efforts; they felt that everything must go into their own effort and they insisted that their works drivers, once they joined Team Lotus, must agree not to drive for any other marque. Seppi certainly gave precedence to Formula One, but not to the point of giving up altogether on sports cars which had played so large a part in building up his reputation. Porsche were not sitting around while Seppi made up his mind: for some time Rico Steinemann had been in touch with Brabham and was suggesting that he sign up Seppi. But with the arrival of Rolf Stommelen the Australian constructor's team was finally made up.

For the Stuttgart factory, Ferrari was obviously the big danger: Maranello could offer both a Formula One car and a worthwhile sports car — that is to say, exactly what Seppi wanted. Still absolutely set on the idea that Siffert should drive a Ferrari, Franco Lini was not inactive, far from it. He telephoned Modena incessantly, trying to persuade the Commendatore. The title won by Porsche thanks to Siffert constituted an extra argument, the more so as Redman had declared that he was ready to follow his Number One. And while Franco was talking to Italy, Rico was in touch with Ferdinand Piech in Stuttgart. The two rivals also had their contacts: Gerard Crombac kept Rico informed of what

Franco was up to, and another journalist kept Franco up to date on Rico.

And while all this was going on, Seppi was getting himself ready for the Mexican Grand Prix. His attitude had not changed and he did not try to conceal his views: 'I am very happy with Porsche and I don't at all want to leave, but I must be sure of a good Formula One drive.'

Porsche took this as read; they must find him a competitive Formula One car. The choice was not very wide. The BRM offer remained, and then there was also the March, a new venture which had already gained the confidence of Ken Tyrrell and Jackie Stewart . . .

As at Watkins Glen, the race did not last long for Siffert: on the fourth lap a shunt with Piers Courage forced him out of the race. The end of the season was in marked contrast to the beginning. Joseph finished up ninth in the world championship with fifteen points.

After the race, Franco and Rico got back to their telephoning. And while Piech was being told how things were working out, Franco failed to persuade Enzo Ferrari to give his agreement over the telephone. That evening, just as in 1968, Seppi told him that he could not wait any longer and that he would stay with Porsche.

Franco was as disappointed as Rico was jubilant. Then all of them, Seppi, Rob, Franco, Rico and all the others, found themselves at Acapulco at a fantastic feast. At 2 o'clock in the morning, on the Place Mariani, surrounded by guitar players, the party laughed and sang. Franco bore no malice toward anyone: 'After all, we are all friends and that's all there is to it,' he summed up.

Joseph himself was by no means at the end of his troubles; he still had to decide between the BRM and the March. At Riverside he met Louis Stanley whose offer was certainly an interesting one, but for four years the BRM had not turned in any results. Seppi felt himself more attracted to the new marque, which had very limited resources but which Porsche would assist financially. In the end, Jo Siffert opted for the March firm, for which he would drive on equal terms with his old friend and rival Chris Amon.

Rob Walker was terribly disappointed; after five years of friendly and successful partnership during which he had come to regard Seppi almost as a son, Seppi was leaving him. But Seppi had got a works contract which to him was very valuable. 'If I had known that Porsche were supporting him financially, I would have helped personally,' he told me later.

Rob and Seppi were not alone in regretting the parting: everyone in the world of motor racing was suprised by it. Rob had always been there, ready to advise, sharing Seppi's burdens and leaving him free to express himself and blossom out. Rob Walker had done everything to make it easier for Jo Siffert to penetrate and progress in the strangely isolated world of Formula One.

On the 9th November, by coming fourth at College Station in Texas, Siffert made sure of a fourth place in the general classification of the Can-Am Series, which would also bring him in a useful sum in dollars.

And so the season came to an end. One thing was now certain; in Formula One, in sports car racing, and in the Can-Am Series the Swiss had shown that he was a redoubtable adversary, among the best drivers of the world.

Siffert was not unaware of his value; he certainly knew what he was up to when he came to renew his contract with Porsche. Seppi managed to get the largest retainer ever paid to a driver for long-distance events.

A good businessman, and a man of his word, Siffert discussed his fee for once and for all — then it was settled. 'Some of the other drivers would sell themselves below their value and then make a further claim at the end of the year,' Rico Steinemann told me one day.

If competition could be said to be over for the year, Jo

Seppi and Veronique

Simone and Seppi

The Italian Grand Prix at Monza, 1970—the heat was tremendous

15th August 1971: At the wheel of the BRM P160, Jo Siffert wins the Austrian Grand Prix at Zeltw

Last journey: the funeral procession passing through the streets of Fribourg

Siffert was not looking forward to a quiet time in Fribourg; his garage and commercial activities were all booming. In addition, his divorce from Sabine had not yet been finalised and Seppi was being asked on all sides to help or take part in various promotions. So it was that on the 5th December he found himself driving a go-kart at the Palais des Sports in Berlin for the traditional sporting soiree. After he had finished a turn of the speedway, his kart shot up the wall, trying to avoid the crowd, and crashed over the top — the gates onto the speedway had been opened too soon. It was a bad knock and Joseph broke his right leg. Luckily, the season was over! It started again, however, in a month's time, in January 1970, with the Argentine Temporada Series in which Seppi was counting on appearing.

The invalid listened attentively to the advice of the celebrated Doctor Martin in Lausanne, the top medical man for Swiss sportsmen, and himself an Olympic medallist. I drove Joseph over to see him once a week. 'Today surely he'll take off the plaster,' Seppi told me, each time we made the trip after the second visit. And each time, on the return journey, I tried to reason with him, telling him that with the best will in the world his bones could not mend as quickly as you could weld together two bits of metal.

Joseph bore his misfortune with patience. He even took the opportunity to relax and look back over his achievements of the year before. In Europe, America, South Africa and the Far East, the Swiss driver had run in thirty-six races over 20,000 miles. 'I spend more time in my racing car than I do in my own personal car,' he told me with some pride. Siffert nearly always travelled by air, and his flying time was also impressive: over 400 hours, or more than 17 days, had been spent in the air in one year. 'I really think I've spent more time in aeroplanes than I did at home,' he wound up.

A great habitue of airports, Seppi knew all sorts of dodges: unlisted numbers, special addresses, which enabled him to fly at the last minute, even without a reservation; or how to hold up an aeroplane for several minutes. 'Monsieur Siffert' was a customer to look after . . .

And he never missed a chance to put his foot on the scale when his suitcase was overweight and he could avoid a surcharge. The old days when he had weighed up the rags were not forgotten so easily.

CHAPTER EIGHT

Porsche's arrangements for the endurance races were decided at the beginning of 1970. The Stuttgart works were still determined to defend their world title but the organization of entry of the cars was going to be looked after by John Wyer's British team, whose reputation had been justly earned. John Wyer would run two Porsche 917s in each race, crewed by Pedro Rodriguez and Leo Kinnunen in one and by Jo Siffert and Brian Redman in the other. As the Mexican and the Finn were both signed up with Wyer's team direct, Seppi and Brian would remain officially Porsche drivers on loan to Wyer from the constructor.

Joseph's right leg was only just all right for the 31st January and the 24-Hour Race at Daytona Beach. Although he was in some pain, he refused the offer of an injection: 'When you really get going, you need all the sensitivity you've got in your head and feet.'

The race was most uncertain. After leading for several hours, Siffert and Redman had to stop four times in four successive laps to repair the suspension. Then the petrol filter got blocked by a foreign body, a shock absorber went, and finally the clutch as well. With an hour to go, Rodriguez was in the lead and Siffert was third, 45 seconds behind the Ferrari of Mario Andretti. The Swiss was in a fighting mood and he moved heaven and earth to make up for the lost time, finally finishing the race in second place, 15 seconds up on the Italo-American combine. In the first race of the season, Team Wyer had pulled off a double but the difficulties throughout the 24-hours did not lead them to suppose that this year's Manufacturers' World Championship would fall to them as easily as the last one.

The appearance on the scene of the new March for the South African Grand Prix did not pass entirely unnoticed, particularly as the youthful British Marque was represented by no less than five cars: two works cars; two wearing the colours of Ken Tyrrell; and a last one for Mario Andretti, who performed a spectacular skid in practice. Things looked good otherwise as Stewart and Amon turned in fastest time on their new machines with 1 minute 19.3 seconds.

Siffert himself was ninth. He liked the car but it seemed to him a bit heavy, the more so as the engine was not developing its full power. After a good start, the Swiss fought a long duel with Ickx for sixth place, but a spin on the 54th lap — it was an 80-lap race — cost him any chance of his first point of the year, and he finished the race in tenth position.

The Ferrari threat was unleashed a fortnight later at Sebring when Andretti and Merzario carried off the famous 12-Hour Race. One after the other, the Porsches fell victim to troubles arising from their hub carriers which were made of a new metal alloy and were not strong enough. Running neck and neck with Rodriguez and Kinnunen in the other car for most of the race, Siffert finished fourth. The Swiss had also set up a new lap record for the circuit at an average speed of over 122 mph.

For the Spanish Grand Prix held this year on the Jarama circuit near Madrid, Siffert was faced with a real nightmare: not all the drivers were given the right to start and for those who were not granted this favour there were only two half-hour sessions for them to gain a place on the grid according to merit — no matter what times they turned in during the ordinary official practice.

After clocking in eleventh best time in ordinary practice, Siffert's March developed a few troubles with the anti-roll bar during the special period set aside for qualifying laps. Rob Walker, who still closely followed the efforts of his former team driver, upbraided the March mechanics: 'Ken Tyrrell has had the rear cross-member of the suspension on Jackie Stewart's March strengthened,' he told them, to encourage them to do the same.

The next day, the second qualifying period was stopped prematurely when Piers Courage's de Tomaso went off the track. At seven in the evening the organizers allotted a further ten minutes of qualifying practice; already partially stripped down for final adjustments before the race, Siffert's car could not take part. So, in spite of having turned in the eleventh best time, the Swiss could not start in the race.

Rob Walker once again intervened and launched a petition that 20 cars should be allowed to start instead of the 17 already admitted. All the teams except one signed, and so did all the drivers. The race directors did not say no, and so shortly before the start, the cars all took their places on the grid. However, with five minutes to go, two officials approached the Swiss driver's March and told him that he had not finally qualified. Siffert could not really believe it until he was grabbed and pulled out of the cockpit of his car. Not to allow him to race was the worst thing that anyone could do to him. A row broke out at once. Furious, Seppi handed out a few violent blows toward the officials but the verdict stood: the victor of the British Grand Prix of 1968 was not allowed to start.

'When one knows with what attention to detail each factory and each driver prepares for a Grand Prix, and what organization of men and materials is involved, it makes one completely despair for the cause of motor racing!' Seppi told me, still spitting with rage.

Fortune hardly smiled on him the following Saturday for

165

the 1000-Kilometre race at Monza. At the beginning of the race a slow car pulled out in the Lesmo corner just as Seppi was overtaking; the Porsche 917 was hit and the suspension broken. Repairs took too long to leave them any hope of winning and the Siffert/Redman partnership ended up in twelfth place.

If relations between Jo and Brian were excellent, they were not quite as good with David Yorke, manager of the Wyer team, who simply did not understand the private code of the two drivers lent by the works. 'When I wanted to know something, I would ask Siffert, not Yorke,' Brian Redman told me later.

The two drivers had one particular convention: Brian would always be ready to take over the wheel on each stage, but Seppi would decide if he would hand over or continue himself. At Monza, Brian, already wearing his helmet, stood by; Joseph made him the sign that he was going on. The British driver withdrew, although the manager had ordered the relief. 'I know you couldn't understand the way we operate,' the driver said calmly to David Yorke — who was an extremely competent man with a lot of experience but who simply was not used to such goings-on.

The next day, Joseph took part for the second time in the hill-climb at Fribourg; in front of his own special public at the wheel of a Formula One Brabham Repco he knocked over three seconds off his own record for the course.

The Siffert/Redman partnership's luck changed at last on the Sunday for the Targa Florio — run over eleven laps of the 45-mile long circuit in the mountains of Sicily. Driving a Porsche 908/3 specially prepared for this very tough race, the Anglo-Swiss team carried off the victory in front of the Rodriguez/Kinnunen crew. Siffert was all the more pleased because the Targa Florio was just about the only Sicilian race which did not feature on his list of successes; the only other real gap that still remained among the races which counted for the Sports Car Manufacturers' World Championship was the Le Mans 24-hour Race.

Siffert still had some worries about qualifying for Monaco, but not for long. The March engine ran well and he managed to get himself safely on to the 6th row of the grid. The race was not exciting. Ickx, Beltoise, Stewart and Amon all had troubles; then Siffert outdid Courage, Pescarolo and Hulme to move into third place by lap 60 — the race was run over 80 laps. Jochen Rindt, who was following Jack Brabham, felt that the March was becoming a threat to him, so he decided to press on and open up a wider gap. At that point a tiresome little fault on Siffert's car intervened: a small aluminium fuel pipe broke. Suffering from fuel starvation, the engine began to misfire.

Some five laps to go and Siffert's car was down to a crawl. As he went through Ste Devote he had to swing the car from side to side to get any fuel through, moving at a snail's place. And just as he was in the middle of the corner, Brabham came up in the lead and only just avoided hitting him. Siffert did not immediately realise that Brabham was trying to pass and because of this, and other difficulties with back markers, Brabham lost five vital seconds on that one lap.

With Rindt's Lotus breathing down his neck, on the last lap Brabham flunked the last corner, the Gasworks Hairpin, and left Rindt the winner. 'My victory? I owe a good deal to Siffert,' Rindt said on television the next day. 'It was his come-back which made me increase speed; if it hadn't been for that, I would have settled for second place and Brabham would certainly not have left his braking too late at the Gasworks.'

Joseph was terribly disappointed, particularly as Rindt on the last lap had broken the lap record set up by Siffert when he made his challenge. But a business deal turned up which soon made him forget his disappointment. Apparently the American Solar Company who were soon to start filming the

24-Hours of Le Mans with Steve McQueen, wanted to buy or hire some racing cars and in particular, two Chevrons. They got in touch with Seppi who said he had got everything they wanted and would hire it all to them. The contract was signed at Spa during the 1000-Kilometre race meeting. The Siffert organization was alerted; they had just one week to find all the promised cars, of which Siffert already possessed only two or three. Paul was put in charge of the operation. In four days, by means of the telephone, he had managed to rake up everything they needed. The two Chevrons, essential to the plot, were not obtained without difficulty: Siffert had to agree to take on an exclusive agency on the Continent for the new British marque.

The contract was signed when they got to Spa: Siffert produced a Porsche 908, four Porsche 911Rs, two Chevrons, one Corvette and a Porsche 914/6; on top of that he supplied ten drivers recruited from among his friends and enough mechanics to keep the cars for six months. As for the cost, that had been totted up by Siffert on the basis of an important American release . . .

'They rather clutched at their whiskies, in which they had hoped to find oblivion, but they hadn't any choice,' Seppi told me later, although he was himself carrying all the risk of mechanical failure.

Joseph could then concentrate exclusively on his racing — and last year after all he had won. He had two bad moments in practice, when twice at over 210 mph, on the sharp descent at the end of the Masta straight, the left rear tyre detached itself — it took over half a mile to stop, he told me. Then, a similar mishap occurred when Redman was driving and they discovered the reason. Under the effects of centrifugal force and friction, the tyres were slipping right out of the rims — all they had to do was to increase the height of the rim by half a centimetre.

On the race day, Siffert and Rodriguez shared the front

row on their two Porsche 917s from the John Wyer team. Each with the same acceleration, the two drivers found themselves side by side going into double bend of Eau Rouge; as he was on the outside, Seppi refused to give way in the first bend. The two Porsches just touched. Now it was Pedro's turn to find himself on the outside coming out of the S — and now he refused to lift his foot. This time the two Porsches really went into each other and went through door to door. The two men's will to win had almost succeeded in eliminating both Porsches in the first 500 yards of the 1000-Kilometre race.

'It was not so much a battle of drivers as a conflict of personalities,' Franco Lini commented.

After tyre trouble, the Rodriguez/Kinnunen partnership did not finish the race, but another merciless duel had opened up between Siffert and Redman and the Ickx/Surtees Ferrari which at one stage managed to collar the lead. However the Belgian driver's team-mate was not on his best form and Redman, always at home at Spa, re-took the Ferrari. For the second time running the Anglo-Swiss partnership won the race at an average speed of 150 mph on the fastest circuit in Europe. Pedro Rodriguez had to console himself with a new lap record which he set up at a fantastic average speed of over 160 mph.

After just enough time to savour this new success, Joseph and Simone went to London where they were going to be married on the 21st May. Rob and Betty Walker had everything laid on. Although he no longer carried the blue and white colours, Seppi was always their friend.

Jo Siffert did not pull off a triple at the Nurburgring: a sudden loss of oil pressure forced him to retire in mid-race when he was in the lead. The March engine did not do much better in the Belgian Grand Prix in which Seppi finished seventh, just missing his first championship point of the year.

He desperately wanted to chalk up a win in the one

long-distance race that still eluded him, and Seppi's chances in the Le Mans 24-Hour Race did seem good. Third at the start, the Swiss took the lead after the second hour. Careful not to over-stress their engine, Siffert and Redman had a comfortable lead over the Porsches of Elford/Ahrens and Attwood/Herrmann. But at the beginning of the eleventh hour the engine suddenly blew up as the leading cars were passing the pits. Hope went up in smoke, leaving only disappointment.

Another even sadder event clouded the following Sunday: after Bruce McLaren, who had lost his life just recently during a private practice session at Goodwood, Piers Courage was also killed driving his de Tomaso Ford on lap 23 of the Dutch Grand Prix at Zandvoort.

Although the risks which they always have to run must prove fatal for a number of them, the Formula One drivers are still very much affected by the news of the death of one of their number. 'Our characters and interests are often widely different, but we are all friends who love and practise the same profession; the death of a friend is always very sad. And for us, who live on the limit, there is each time the question: who will be next?' Seppi told me.

The next Sunday he was in his BMW for the start of the Formula Two Grand Prix of Rouen. Leader of the European Championship, a second Swiss was on the start-line, Clay Regazzoni, a Tecno works driver, who had just been signed up for Formula One by Ferrari. His first outing for Ferrari had been a success — he had come fourth in the Dutch Grand Prix the week before.

Joseph soon got into the lead, setting a cracking pace; the experts in Formula Two snapped at his heels and would not let him go. Regazzoni, the young Brazilian Emerson Fittipaldi, the Australian Tim Schenken, the Swede Ronnie Peterson, the two British drivers Derek Bell and Peter Westbury. It was a crazy battle. Siffert fought off the continuous and concerted attacks of the pack behind him. And the old fox pulled it off; he crossed the line half a length ahead of Regazzoni and Fittipaldi.

The March was still giving trouble a week later for the French Grand Prix held at Clermont-Ferrand. The car was not going well and the Swiss did not seem to be in the running. On the 24th of the 38 laps, at the start of the left-hander on the rise just before track runs back to the pits, the brakes locked just for an instant; Siffert fought for control of his machine but the March, which understeered badly, ploughed into the safety barrier. 'I thought I had broken a leg,' Seppi told me, when I found him in hospital in the middle of a massage. Luckily the chassis of the March was not tubular, or things might have been a great deal more serious.

In Switzerland, the public began to get worried: after six races, Siffert had not scored one point in the world championship. His reputation as a car-breaker, acquired during the Cooper-Maserati period, bobbed up to the surface again. Others thought that the Fribourgeois was getting old and that it was perhaps time for him to give up racing, and then there was always Clay Regazzoni — another Swiss . . .

'The day that I felt the slightest falling away I would hang up my helmet at once, and for good,' Seppi told me when I passed on to him what I had been hearing around the place — things which did not get to him direct. 'You know, the great thing is that they are talking about it; it's only when they don't talk any more that things become really worrying. And again, those who criticise the most are usually the people who have never seen a race in their lives!'

Next weekend, at Watkins Glen, in the 500-Kilometres of New York, Jo Siffert showed once again that a good machine could make him a formidable adversary: with Brian Redman he finished second in the 6-Hour Race, driving the John Wyer Porsche 917, and next day in the same car he started in a

Can-Am race and also finished second, only 28 seconds behind Denny Hulme on the 7-litre McLaren Chevrolet.

Staged at Brands Hatch, the British Grand Prix did not bear much resemblance to the race which Siffert and Amon had enlivened two years before. Wearing the colours of the same works team, the Swiss and the New Zealander lapped much less quickly than some of the privately-entered Marchs. In the race Amon finished fifth, and Jochen Rindt won by a lucky chance after Brabham had run out of fuel just 500 yards from the finish when comfortably in the lead. Siffert retired after 22 laps with a broken hub carrier, after having climbed through the field from twentieth to tenth place.

In the German Grand Prix which was held that year at Hockenheim, the directors of March really had something to worry about: in spite of all their efforts, Siffert had still not qualified and only one short practice session remained. All the works mechanics were clustered around the March to try and make it go better. And it seemed to do the trick: Siffert turned in a lap of 2 minutes 0.00 seconds which was the fourth fastest and put him in the second row of the grid beside Regazzoni. Although it was official, the time was not really correct — the majority of the team had clocked him in at 2 minutes 01.0 seconds. 'I thought that Seppi had certainly benefited from a timekeeper's error, but it was the first bit of luck he'd had this year in Formula One and we could not help being pleased about it,' Rob told me. His driver, Graham Hill, had also been having his troubles at the wheel of Siffert's old Lotus.

More than 100,000 spectators packed the extraordinary stands of Hockenheim on the day of the race, and among them several thousands of Swiss waving little red and white flags. Siffert and Regazzoni received a tremendous ovation. When they got back to the pits, Seppi came up to me: 'What do you think, I've just seen my father.'

'Oh good, I haven't seen him — was he behind the pits?'

'No, I just saw him by chance among that enormous crowd in the stands! He was waving a Swiss flag. It's rather sad, I couldn't let him know that I had spotted him.'

Joseph kept in touch with the leading bunch with Jacky Ickx's Ferrari in the front of it for several laps, but then his less powerful engine forced him to ease up a bit. Then, three laps from the end, when he was still holding fifth place, the engine failed and he was out of the race. Even so, Seppi was classified seventh but at the end of the eighth round in the world championship he had still not scored any points.

The most disappointed of his supporters was certainly his young nephew Mark, to whom Joseph had promised a bike when he scored his first point.

'Tonton, you must go faster!' the small boy of five told the racing driver.

In the Austrian Grand Prix, for once Jo Siffert's March made it to the end and finished ninth as Jacky Ickx on the Ferrari was making his lap of honour. The 12-cylinder cars had made all the running on the Zeltweg circuit — two Ferraris, two BRMS and a Matra had taken the first five places.

The prodigies which he and Amon had had to achieve to finish even one lap had more to do with tightrope-walking than with driving. 'What they achieved at the wheels of those two trucks was fantastic,' wrote an Italian journalist.

After the race Seppi bumped into Franco Lini: 'I thought of you several times during the race,' he told him.

'Why? Did you see me out on the circuit?' asked the journalist.

'No, but as I was driving I said to myself: "Ah, if I had listened to Franco I would be battling away at the front of the pack on a Ferrari!" '

Soon after Chris Amon also ran into Lini and had much the same to say. The New Zealand driver had really been very unlucky: the year before he had been racing for Maranello and had quit because he thought he would do better with the Ford-Cosworth engine.

173

Amon was not on very good terms with the March management with whom he communicated as little as possible, but in contrast he got on perfectly well with Seppi as did everyone else. 'I never heard anyone speak badly of him,' he told me later.

This quality of Siffert's was recognised and appreciated: when he had something to say, to make a complaint, he would always address himself to the person concerned and would sort out his differences man to man.

The last practice for the Italian Grand Prix was a tragedy: the leader in the world championship, Jochen Rindt, went off the track going into Parabolica and was killed at the wheel of his Lotus which crashed into the safety barrier.

Although everyone in the pits knew of the tragic end of the leading Lotus driver, the other drivers were not told of the death of their colleague. The sad news was not announced until after practice at a session of the GPDA.

On the way to the meeting, to which I went with Seppi, he told me that he had just made fourth best time and would start on the first row of the grid beside Jack Brabham. 'I gather that Rindt may not start,' he said. 'His car was apparently badly damaged.'

'I don't know, I haven't seen it,' I mumbled, not daring to break the news to him.

Badly hit by Jochen's death, Seppi spoke to me about it a little just before the start of the race: 'Drivers should refuse to race cars which are not sufficiently proved. We already refuse to drive on doubtful circuits. But then we always want to go faster. The engineers will have to discover some new alloy and lighten the cars as much as possible. But really there is no proper solution,' he added.

Siffert's race was a short one: on the second lap he came round last, running very slowly, one arm raised. The engine had blown up. 'Pity, for once the car was well set up,' he said after he had walked back to the pits.

174

At the end of a fantastic race, Clay Regazzoni won the Italian Grand Prix at Monza. In Switzerland, influenced by a section of the Press, some people thought that a rivalry beyond the field of sport had sprung up between Seppi and Clay. In fact, there was nothing of the sort. The two men were good friends. If they were very much in competition on the racetrack, it stopped there.

'It's a good thing for Switzerland to have more than one Formula One driver,' said the Fribourgeois. 'Perhaps that may decide the authorities to allow a motor racing circuit in Switzerland . . . '

After a further setback in Canada, Siffert finished ninth in the US Grand Prix where the transfer game began. Without wanting to knock March, Seppi did not conceal his intention to quit the youthful English firm and some offers had already been made to him. The problem was less acute than in the two preceding years; his next contract for endurance races would be signed direct with John Wyer and no longer with the Stuttgart works. BRM had a good chance of acquiring the services of the Fribourgeois on condition, however, first of all, that certain difficulties over advertising were sorted out.

The last endurance race in the calendar for the Sports Car Constructors' World Championship was the 1000-Kilometre Race at Zeltweg in Austria, and Seppi took the opportunity to bring to an end his run of bad luck which had lasted for several months. Driving for the last time with Brian Redman — who had decided to give up all competitive driving and go and settle in South Africa — Siffert again won the Austrian race.

Attaching great importance to the human qualities of his co-driver, Seppi tried to find a replacement for Brian whose retirement he very much regretted. His choice fell on another Briton, Derek Bell, a thirty-year-old driver who had just come second in the Formula Two Trophy of Europe, behind Regazzoni. Cool, reserved and quick, Derek accepted at once.

For once Joseph spent the next weekend with his family at home at Belfaux near Fribourg, but Seppi did not enjoy peace and quiet for long. A little while before, he had bought a motocross motorbike for his Sunday sport . . .

At about this time, the Fribourg driver was sent a calendar for 1971, illustrated with pictures of motor racing. One of the pictures showed Siffert with Rindt, Courage and McLaren at the Monaco Grand Prix. 'Have you noticed?' he said to me, 'The photograph was only taken six months ago, and of the four drivers I am the only one still alive. It really is an offbeat profession.'

Although he did not ignore it, Siffert spoke as little as possible about death. Perhaps he lived too close to it. And then, he so much loved life, his own life.

At the Mexican Grand Prix, after the two March works drivers had had three engines blow up in three days, the main surprise for Siffert was not his retirement but the disappearance of his helmet, snitched by some person unknown at the beginning of the first practice session. By chance, Emerson Fittipaldi had a spare and by a further bit of good luck a Japanese journalist had in a pocket some white adhesive tape which Seppi cut up to form a Swiss cross and stuck on to the front.

And so the Formula One season came to an end and for the first time since 1962 the name of Jo Siffert did not feature in the general classification of the Drivers' World Championship.

The Swiss driver was terribly disappointed but he preferred not to think about it.

'I'll try and forget all about this year and make a fresh start,' he told his friends.

Soon afterwards, he bought from the factory the March which had been the cause of so much disappointment during the season. Properly set up the car was not as bad as all that. The real problem was to get a strong enough engine. Then the car could be put to very good use in less important races, or hired out to people. Already Joseph had an idea . . .

Entered in the Kyalami 9-Hour Race which he finished in second place, teamed with Kurt Ahrens, 27 seconds behind Jacky Ickx's Ferrari, Jo Siffert finished the season at Kyalami where he had started in March — driving a March in the South African Grand Prix.

The official announcement of his engagements for 1971 was not made until the 11th November. He would race the next year for BRM in Formula One; for John Wyer in sports car events, sharing a Porsche 917 with Derek Bell; Siffert would only enter a few Formula Two races driving a Chevron which he would enter under his own colours.

CHAPTER NINE

Newly inscribed in the calendar for the Manufacturers' World Championship, the Buenos Aires 1000-Kilometre Race was the first rendezvous of the year for the sports car drivers. Third in practice, Joseph Siffert was also for the first time starting a race crewed with Derek Bell. The race itself was saddened by the fatal accident of Ignazio Giunti during the first refuelling; he was leading and went at full speed into the Beltoise Matra which had run out of fuel and was being pushed along the track. The race was not stopped and the Siffert/Bell partnership gave Team Wyer its first victory of the season.

On his return to Switzerland, Joseph was busy with his business affairs and a week later he again took a plane to Buenos Aires where he was competing in the Formula One Argentine Grand Prix. The race did not yet count for the World Championship, and BRM had decided not to take part. But Seppi himself entered the March he had bought from the works. Now the Chief Foreman of Jo Siffert Automobiles, Jean-Pierre Oberson still put in to go to South America as a race mechanic. Coming in first in the first heat, Siffert had a few troubles in the second and only came sixth in the final classification. The best place he had ever achieved driving the March!

From there, Siffert went straight on to Florida for the 24-Hour Race at Daytona Beach. On the day of the race, as he was leaving the hotel to go to the circuit, somebody handed him a telegram which he stuffed into a pocket of his overalls without looking at it. Just before the start of the race, Derek asked him: 'Was it a girl or a boy?'

'I don't know, I haven't heard yet,'

'But the telegram — was it something else?'

'Of course — I haven't opened it — perhaps that's what it is!'

And so Seppi discovered that a few hours before he had become the father of a little boy, whose name would be Philippe, and that mother and child were both doing well. Suddenly, his interest in the race was a little subdued. Nevertheless, Siffert quickly took command, but retired after four hours when the new 5-litre engine blew up — it seemed to be more delicate than the old 4.5-litre.

From Daytona Siffert went on to Bogota where the first Colombian Grand Prix for Formula Two was due to take place. The Fribourgeois had entered two Chevrons; his own and one which he had just sold to Xavier Perrot, another Swiss driver. With a new Cosworth engine, of which the mechanics had had to re-do all the valves during the night before the race, Jo Siffert won: the enthusiasm for his victory was terrific. The South Americans laid on a party, the like of which Seppi had never seen before. The next Sunday, the City of Bogota had its own race over the same circuit; once cannot become a habit and the Swiss decided not to go home. His stay was not exactly restful: Corrida, receptions, crocodile-hunts and stomach-aches were the main highlights.

Joseph was outright favourite for the next race of which he won the first heat, but his distributor broke ten laps from the end of the second and he had to make do with a second place in the final classification, behind the German driver, Rolf Stommelen.

Three weeks later, in South Africa, Siffert was at last installed behind the wheel of a Formula One V12 BRM whose colours he would defend throughout the season together with Pedro Rodriguez. The Mexican and the Swiss, whom some people thought of as implacable foes, thus found themselves in the same team, both for Formula One and for sports cars. This rivalry in fact was really more an identity of character: in both men there was the same thoughtful temperament, the will to win regardless of speed. Apart from the odd incidents due to their intolerance of each other on the circuit, Pedro and Joseph got on perfectly well but not for too long; pointed in the same direction their characters were too strongly defined for them ever to be real friends.

In spite of his retirement a little before halfway because of his engine overheating — an ailment which affected all the BRMs at Kyalami — Siffert was very pleased with his first real outing. Fast and light, the BRM was certainly not perfectly set up yet, but he was quite sure that when it was he would pick up a few places at the finishing line. 'It's a long time since I had a go with the leading bunch in a world championship race,' Seppi told me fifteen hours after the race when he was already back in Fribourg.

The Sebring 12-Hour Race was rather active for the Siffert/Bell partnership: in the lead after two hours of racing, their Porsche 917 suddenly ran out of petrol on the circuit. Siffert then climbed onto the back seat of an official's motorbike who took him back to the pits for a can of petrol, returning him by the same means of locomotion. The cost of the operation was, however, high — Siffert had lost 19 laps, plus a further penalty of 4 laps for having used two wheels rather than two feet in the relief operation. The delay was too much to make up and the Siffert/Bell car finished in fifth place. The Swiss driver had however put in fastest lap, beating at the same time his own official lap record for the circuit, this time with a speed of 124.43 mph.

The Questor Grand Prix for Formula One was run the following Sunday in California and although it did not count for the world championship most of the cars turned up. At the wheel of a new BRM, the P60, Siffert in spite of breaking part of the suspension five laps from the end, took a promising sixth place.

The Easter holiday was rather hectic: after the 1000-Kilometre race at Brands Hatch which Siffert and Bell finished in third place after some trouble with the brakes and a delay while he fixed the spare wheel which had come off, Siffert lined up at Oulton Park on the Good Friday for a Formula One race. But for this race Joseph was not only a driver; he had also entered his March and entrusted the driving to Alan Rollinson. When a tyre on the BRM went flat at the moment of starting, the March ran a steady race to finish in fifth place.

The next meeting was three days later on Easter Monday at Thruxton where Seppi competed in two races: a Formula Two on the Chevron in which he retired, and a sports car race which he won on the Porsche 917. Rob Walker lived not so far away, at Nunney and Seppi and Simone stayed with him; Stirling Moss was also a house guest. The two drivers, the old and the new, talked together a lot during their short stay. Each seemed to both like and admire the other, and Rob was delighted to have the two drivers he liked most as guests.

Just about the first person I saw when I arrived at Barcelona airport was a man in driving overalls carrying a leather grip in which I could just make out a red helmet. It was Friday evening, and two days later would be the Spanish Grand Prix, the second round in the World Championship, on the Montjuich circuit where the first practice had taken place that day.

'Hurry up, dump your suitcase and come back here. We're off immediately for Le Mans,' Seppi told me.

No sooner said than done, and a quarter of an hour later I found myself in a private plane from the Porsche works bound for Tours where we landed three hours later. From there we went to Le Chartre-sur-le-Loir where Team Wyer had booked rooms. Tomorrow the first practice would be held for the 24-Hours of Le Mans. Saturday morning at 9 o'clock Seppi was ready to go out on the track; there wasn't much time to spare — in four hours he would have to try and bring up to scratch four different Porsches, checking up on their form, aerodynamics, length and general tune. A bit of anxious waiting — no car could go out unless the official doctor was there, and naturally he turned up a bit late — and Seppi was off. Let loose, he lowered the lap record each time round. Stopping either to give the engineer, Falk, his impressions — a taciturn man, Falk and Seppi understand each other to perfection — or to change cars, the driver wasted no time at all except once to ask me to buy some food and drink for the flight back.

Suddenly the loudspeaker announced a new official lap record in 3 minutes 17 seconds at an average speed of 155 mph which meant a top speed down the Mulsanne Straight of something like 250 mph. 'With an average speed like that, I should qualify at Indianapolis,' Seppi commented briefly.

At five minutes past one the driver climbed out of the fourth Porsche and a car drove us to Le Mans airport; we took off twenty minutes later. A quick sandwich and Joseph was asleep. Over the Pyrenees a violent storm terribly shook up the little Porsche plane in which we were the only two passengers. Seeing my anxiety Seppi, finally woken up by the shaking, pretended to talk to himself: 'I always though I would end up crashing in one of these cuckoos', he grumbled into his moustache. A quick sideways look and I felt better; then he roared with laughter. We got to Barcelona just before five and went straight to the circuit where he would run in the last Formula One practice. As if his day had only just started, Seppi installed himself in the cockpit of his BRM. Then the rain came down and completely mucked up this last session: nobody improved on their times. In the race the next day a wrongly adjusted bolt in the driveshaft of the gearbox forced Siffert to retire on the sixth lap.

Two days later, in Fribourg, the Press were invited to the garage to the official unveiling of 'Jo Siffert Automobiles Racing.' This new team would in future enter two Chevrons for which Joseph was the exclusive European agent, entrusted to Gerard Larrousse for the European Constructors' Championship in the up to 2-litre class, and to Francois Mazet, another Frenchman, for Formula Two when Siffert was not available. In addition the March would also take part in some Formula One races with a driver specially appointed for each race. Apart from this, Jo Siffert Automobiles Racing, of which Paul Blancpain was the manager, would look after a collection of cars ranging from a Porsche 917 to a 1925 Bugatti which would be available on hire for exhibitions or promotional activities and so on.

Second in the 1000-Kilometre race at Monza, behind the Rodriguez/Oliver car, the Siffert/Bell partnership hoped to reverse this order in the next 1000-Kilometre race at Spa Francorchamps — Seppi had won this race in the two preceding years.

Joseph and Pedro were only there for the first practice on Thursday. With just time to get their hand in, the two drivers flew to England where, on the Saturday, they drove their BRMs in the Trophy race at Silverstone. In the meantime, Derek Bell went out and turned in the best outright time in practice 3 minutes 16 seconds — beating the next man, Vic Elford, by over two seconds.

The start was electrifying. Straightaway, Siffert and Rodriguez went out in front and for the first half ran at an average speed of over 155 mph; the gap between the Swiss and the Mexican was never more than one second. It was Seppi who set up a new outright record for the circuit, covering the 8.76 miles in 3 minutes 14.6 seconds at the fantastic average speed of 162.09 mph. 'It's incredible — I wouldn't have thought it was possible to go so fast on this circuit!' Joseph told me on being told of his new record.

In fact it confirmed what Rob Walker had said some years before: 'I think that Seppi is really the best on fast circuits with long bends.'

After refuelling at the 500 kilometre mark, Derek Bell slipped on his first lap which he completed 15 seconds behind Jackie Oliver who had taken over from Rodriguez. Joseph was annoyed, and even more so, when, from the pits, David Yorke made no signal to his co-driver.

Seppi asked me to come with him towards the end of the pits where we borrowed a blackboard. I had my stopwatch and Seppi signalled the gap between Bell and Oliver each time that Derek came past and urged him on to go faster. Derek got going again. After 12 laps he was back on the tail of Pedro's co-driver, but he did not overtake.

Seppi got himself ready for the next refuelling stop when he reckoned to take over the wheel again. But David Yorke refused to let him go out, saying that he had already driven for 500 kilometres. Derek would finish the race. Livid, Seppi joined me at the end of the pits where we made desperate signals to Bell urging him to go for Oliver, but Derek responded each time with a helpless gesture and at the end of the 1000 kilometres the Siffert/Bell car came in second to the Rodriguez/Oliver car in the same time of 4 hours 1 minute 9.7 seconds but half a length behind.

'Wouldn't Oliver let you pass? Why didn't you overtake?' I asked Derek after the finish.

'Yorke told me not to,' the driver replied briefly.

'Not wanting another fratricidal battle between the two Porsches and in view of the supremacy of Team Wyer, the manager had simply decided beforehand in what order they would finish!

For the Targa Florio the following Sunday Joseph was

back with his old co-driver. Unable to live without motor sport, Brian Redman had quit South Africa after five months; as Bell did not know at all the 45-mile mountain circuit in Sicily, Seppi was going to drive once again with Brian.

Adopting a tactic both simple and above all prudent, the John Wyer team manager refused to let Siffert and Rodriguez start together — the risk of a fatal duel was too great. A bit edgy, Brian — who had never started first in the race before — did not get very far: after 20 miles he touched a wall and the machine caught fire instantly. Redman got himself out and rolled into the grass, but his face was caught — the vizor of his helmet melted and he was badly burned. Brought back to the pits by helicopter he was quickly looked after but his burns were, serious enough for him to be taken to hospital.

Remembering his accident in 1964 in Syracuse, Seppi, who had no further interest in the race, wanted at all costs to avoid a similar stay for his friend. He managed to arrange for the Porsche works aircraft to take the injured man to London.

For the Monaco Grand Prix, Siffert travelled in the wake of the unbeatable Jackie Stewart right from the start. But on the 31st lap the Swedish driver, Ronnie Peterson, managed to get the better of the Swiss who seemed to be on his way to a safe third place. Then, three-quarters of the way round, the oil pressure began to fall inexorably and that was that — to the disappointment of the thousands of Swiss present.

The victor at Monza, Porsche looked like getting some of their own medicine on German soil from an Italian car. A Ferrari 312P and an Alfa-Romeo T33/3 occupied the front row of the grid for the 1000-Kilometre race at the Nurburgring — admittedly in front of four Porsche 908/3s. A great deal more at home on the circuit than his team-mate, Siffert took third place behind the two red cars straightaway, but on the seventh of the 44 laps, on the Dottinger Straight, his chassis suddenly broke. Fearing a major setback, David Yorke decided to substitute Siffert for Oliver as Rodriguez's co-driver — Rodriguez was not on his best form and was running some 20 seconds behind the Elford/Larrousse Porsche while the leaders were over a minute ahead. Then, one after the other, towards mid-race, the Alfa and then the Ferrari retired — one with engine trouble and the other suffering from overheating. The struggle was now a family affair between the Porsches of the Martini and John Wyer teams.

Absolutely flat out, which did not prevent him from giving a little wave to the journalist, Georges Descoeudres, and myself, when he spotted us on the vertigious descent of the Hatzenbach, Siffert had almost caught up the Elford/Larrousse car when he handed over the wheel to the Mexican on the last but one refuelling stop, but Rodriguez began to drop back a few seconds.

At the final refuelling stop, when it was still possible to make it if the Swiss took over again, Rodriguez refused to give up the wheel.

Siffert was furious: 'He can do what he likes but not with me!' Siffert told me, and he went straight off without waiting for the end of the race in which Rodriguez only just retained his second place ahead of the Marko/van Lennep Porsche.

Forgetting his displeasure, Siffert flew straight off to England where the next day, Whit Monday, he would run in a Formula Two race at Crystal Palace. Tuesday he was running at Vallelunga near Rome.

The Swiss Press were worried. Was Siffert racing too much? We were only at the 1st of June and already he had run in twenty-two races in the one season. Was he overdoing things a bit?

Joseph himself wasn't worried. His main object in life was to race as much as possible. 'I am only really happy when I am racing,' he would always say. At this time nothing had changed, and without this aspect of his personality he would certainly never have made it to the top in motor sport.

For the ninth time, Siffert was going to compete in mid-June in the 24-Hours of Le Mans. The Swiss driver longed to chalk this one up: if he were to win it, there would be no race in the world championship of marques for which he could not claim a victory.

The last practice session was dramatic: Seppi suddenly pulled into his pit and literally hurled himself out of the cockpit of his Porsche 917L and bounded towards me like a man distracted. 'I should be dead,' he yelled at me, and then turned towards the mechanics; under the influence of nervous shock, Joseph could hardly explain what had happened. As he was going through White House, Seppi had suddenly had his route blocked by a slower car which had not seen him coming. In avoiding it, Siffert had spun off and then proceeded backwards for more than 300 yards, walloped the safety barrier with one side of the car, crossed the track and hit in the same way the barrier on that side, and then by an extraordinary chance fetched up on the track facing in the right direction. He just engaged second gear and drove slowly back.

For half an hour the driver was in a state of delayed shock, trembling violently from the fright he had just experienced. It was not until that evening that he could analyse things clearly. 'I think that the risk is comparable to taking a ski-lift 'I think that the risk is comparable to taking a ski-lift ticket: each ticket gives you one day. But one day there are no more tickets, no more luck, and that's the end. Everyone has a different stock of chances — the bore is not knowing if you have any left. Today, in any case, I used up one ticket!'

This philosophy of chance may perhaps seem over-simplified but the built-in period of grace showed a certain resignation in the driver, conscious of the danger around without being too much of a fatalist.

'And you, when you drive off in your car in the morning, do you think that perhaps you will not return?' Siffert replied one day to someone who asked if he thought about death at the start of a race.

The whole incident was forgotten by the Saturday afternoon at the moment of the start of the race. To conserve his engine as much as possible, Joseph did not force the pace and when Rodriguez and Oliver took the lead, the Porsche Number 17 of Siffert and Bell lapped some 15 seconds slower than its optimum. On the second hour, the Anglo-Swiss team found itself in the lead, however, but then dropped three places to re-fit an electrical connection. This minor bother marked the beginning of a long series of troubles: right through the night of the race the Porsche suffered from a list of defects ranging from trouble with Number 17's lighting, with the wheels, with the brakes which had to be bled, to adjustments to the suspension. Realizing his inevitable defeat, Seppi no longer had the heart to go on racing: 'If this goes on I am going to go and have some beer,' he told me in a filthy temper.

The coup de grace did not come until the early hours of the morning: Bell finally retired for good with a serious crack in the engine block.

Jo Siffert had not failed in everything at Le Mans. His recent discussions with Porsche about an eventual participation by the factory in the Can-Am Series was about to bear fruit. Joseph bought a Porsche 917/10 specially designed which he would personally enter under his own colours in the American Championships.

He still had to find two good mechanics; casing the pits, Seppi made contact with two Swiss, Eddy Wyss and Ugo Schibler — one a specialist in chassis, the other an expert on the preparation of engines and gearboxes. Both men accepted his offer and would join him at Stuttgart as soon as possible to help in the building of the car.

The first race was just over a month ahead, at Watkins Glen

Chez Porsche everyone was delighted with this new idea of Siffert's, for it would open up horizons, particularly as with the 3-litre limit on cylinder capacity on prototypes in 1972, Stuttgart had decided to suspend their participation in the world championship of marques.

After over 22 months of waiting, since the German Grand Prix of 1969, Joseph Siffert at last scored a point in the Drivers' World Championship on the 20th June 1971 when he finished sixth in the Dutch Grand Prix at Zandvoort. His supporters were relieved; but the most delighted of all was certainly his nephew Mark who at last got the bike he had been promised for so long!

However, twenty Grands Prix without one single point was something not easily forgotten; so Joseph did it again a fortnight later at Le Castellet when he took fourth place in the French Grand Prix and also collected three more championship points.

A big party was being held two days later at the house of Bernard Blancpain in the suburbs of Fribourg. Seppi, who was celebrating his thirty-fifth birthday, and Simone were of course among those invited, and their arrival certainly caused something of a stir as Joseph drove up to the house in a Porsche 917 with a fantastic amount of noise. The surprise was general, even Bernard had not been let into the secret. The person most tickled by the operation was perhaps Councillor Nello Celio, the Swiss Minister of Finance, who during the evening discovered in Jo Siffert a character he had not known until then and which surprised him as much as it delighted him.

Jo Siffert had much more to him than one might have expected to find in a racing driver: he was a real ambassador for his country. The image of Switzerland generally is not always a very attractive one to the foreigner; too often it is that of a population of hardworking ants, living without

189

generosity on their mountains and heaps of gold. Wherever he went — those who went around with him and the echoes, heard or written, confirm this — Siffert made his mark on the vague and often unfair idea of Switzerland, adding a different image in which he blended two qualities which are not typically Swiss — humour and panache. Whether they were interested in motor sport or not, nobody who met him could remain indifferent to Jo Siffert.

A new drama unfolded the following Sunday in Germany: Pedro Rodriguez was killed driving a Ferrari during an Inter-Series race on the Norisring near Nuremberg. Seppi, who heard the news at home, was quite overcome. It was because the qualities of the Mexican driver were so similar to his own that Pedro had been his great rival. Joseph felt out on his own. At both BRM and John Wyer, he felt charged with a heavier burden. He was now their sole hope.

For the first time since the Canadian Grand Prix of 1969 Siffert found himself on the front row of the grid in a Formula One race at the British Grand Prix which was run this year at Silverstone. And after five laps the Swiss driver's BRM tucked itself in behind Jackie Stewart who led the race. Surprised, the Scotsman was not happy. Until today he had always thought that Siffert was too temperamental to be considered a top driver — and this to the point that he did not worry himself too much about a slip or a slide when he was running ahead of him. Of course, Seppi together with Ickx was the master of endurance races, but the best drivers did not develop from there. Today, when all the efforts of BRM were concentrated on Siffert, Stewart really began to reckon the Swiss's potential and he was slightly relieved when, after the 15th lap, the BRM began to get steadily smaller in the Tyrrell-Ford's rear view mirror. A victim of the heat, the tyres of Siffert's machine obliged him to steady up a bit.

'If he had not run into troubles, my victory would have

been a great deal harder to come by,' Jackie Stewart said afterwards.

The news of Jo Siffert's participation in the Can-Am Series on a 5-litre Porsche 917/10 burst like a bomb. Nobody in America had expected a small European car to come and mix it with the big monsters of 7- or 8-litres, known as McLarens driven by Hulme and Revson, as a Lola driven by Stewart, or as a Shadow driven by Oliver. They soon got over their surprise and readily accepted the trio of friends — Siffert, Wyss and Schibler — into the American Series, a real dollar waltz.

If he had 100 bhp less, Siffert made up for it to a great extent with his driving skill and from his first race at Watkins Glen he stepped in between the two distinct groups — the good and the less good drivers. The result was decisive: in spite of worrying vibrations, Joseph took third place behind Revson and Hulme and ahead of the 7-litre Ferrari of Mario Andretti.

Siffert showed himself once again a dangerous rival for Stewart in the German Grand Prix. But as he came round on the fourth of the 12 laps, lying second behind the Scotsman, the Swiss made a sign that his brakes were not working properly. Two laps later the ignition coil went and he had to stop for good. For once, his retirement was just as well: on stripping down the car the mechanics discovered that the BRM's chassis was cracked and certainly would not have lasted another lap. Seppi had had a near squeak!

Seppi had invited his mother, whose birthday it was, to come with him to the Austrian GP which would be held on the 11th August on the Zeltweg circuit. At sixty, Maria Siffert was to have her first baptism in the air.

The Swiss had put in sixth best time during the first two practice sessions, but then in the third and last session he really got going and turned in the fastest time of all in the very last two minutes. For the first time since Graham Hill in

1964, also in the Austrian Grand Prix, BRM had a car in pole position. The problems of tyres, of ignition and of over-heating, which BRM had had to face up to the last few times, had not really been resolved, but the climate was one of optimism particularly as some thick cloud had already obscured the sun and reduced a little the stifling heat at the start.

Warding off an attack from Regazzoni, Siffert took command of the race at the start. But Stewart did not waste any time overtaking the Ferrari and glued himself to the BRM, which was quickly registered by the BRM driver. The two men soon outpaced their immediate pursuers — Cevert and Regazzoni. But the Scotsman could not keep up the murderous pace of the Swiss. Siffert was unbeatable. After a few difficulties, Stewart let his team-mate, Cevert, through and he set off after the leader, but the gap was too great for him to close. Unless something went wrong, Siffert could not be caught. And this was even less likely when the two Tyrrells had to retire. Stewart went off the track at about half-time when a driveshaft went; Cevert retired with gearbox trouble. As for the Ferraris, they were not in the running and, 12 laps from the end, the second man was the Brazilian Emerson Fittipaldi on the Lotus.

Suddenly Siffert slowed up a little and began to lose four seconds a lap on the Lotus. In the pits everyone thought that the Swiss wanted to make sure of his victory. But it was nothing of the sort — the BRM was holding the road less and less well, and Seppi thought that the back suspension was going. In fact, a back tyre was slowly deflating. The suspense built up over the last lap and finally, having led from beginning to end over 54 laps, Joseph Siffert won the Austrian Grand Prix in 1 hour 30 minutes 23.91 seconds at an average speed of 132.30 mph, 4.12 seconds in front of Emerson Fittipaldi. The Fribourgeois had set up a new absolute record for the circuit in 1 minute 38.47 seconds at

an average speed of 134.39 mph. His triumph was absolute.
Jackie Stewart who was now certain of the world championship title for 1971 was the first to confirm this: 'Jo was
splendid: in pole position, then in front from start to finish,
with the lap record as well, he certainly led the race as a top
driver!'

The French journalist, Bernard Cahier, was not short of
praise either: 'Even Stewart on one of his better days would
not have beaten him! And then everyone knows how difficult
the Zeltweg circuit is . . . '

As to the person most interested, the winner, he had
vanished. After being garlanded and wildly applauded, Siffert
was literally carried off by Georges Descoeudres who
questioned him for half an hour live on the Radio Suisse
Romande.

Then Joseph went back, not without some difficulty, to
the paddock where thousands of his supporters acclaimed
him, chanting his name. Here he gave a humorous account
of the race to his friends: 'It is rather fun to see the world
champion in your rear view mirror,' he said, delighted and not
really taking in his fantastic achievement.

Rob Walker, for the first time for ages, missed a Grand
Prix and so unfortunately did not see this victory: 'I don't
know if I would have wept with joy for Seppi or with sorrow
at not having played any part in the victory,' he told me
afterwards.

Another man joined us in the caravan; a committed
spectator, he had been on tenterhooks throughout the
race — on this day to know Siffert and to be one of his
closest friends was almost a disadvantage. It was Jean
Tinguely.

Although he did not have at all the competitive spirit, the
sculptor was a passionate devotee of motor sport. Not going
near the pits, he always went racing as a real onlooker, lost in
the crowd. His was a strange world and although he stood

back from the track itself, he felt himself a part of the man and the machine. In the spectacle of racing, the man actually masters the machine but he is also part of it. It has something to do with man's strange search to express his virility which lies behind everything that he undertakes. And there was also a further attraction: the racing driver is not a faceless man in an office — he is an American Indian, a toreador, a man possessed. This all-masculine image of the warrior, noble and beautiful, fascinated Jean, for whom Seppi was the living symbol of motor racing. Often nervous before a race, Joseph was an entirely new and different man at the wheel of his machine. And in giving himself up to this life, with its colourful accessories, Siffert was at once revealing himself on a grand scale as a master, a fool and a child who lives as he pleases.

Jean also fascinated Seppi. Apart from his machines, at once genial and absurd, he saw him with the eye of a realist but from a new angle. Poet, artist, collector, a man who was always cheerful, Joseph found in Jean's innermost heart not only a means of escape but also a place of refuge.

Still cheered by his victory, Seppi flew off three days later to America where he was going to take part in two of the Can-Am races. At Lexington, Ohio, he took advantage of the retirement of the two McLarens of Hulme and Revson to finish second behind the Lola-Chevrolet of Jackie Stewart. The atmosphere of his little team delighted him; it was rather like the old days of Formula Junior. Now the financial problems had gone, or rather they had changed — but the spirit remained the same. At Elkhart Lake in Wisconsin Seppi polished up his Porsche 917/10 which Eddy Wyss and Ugo Schibler were in the middle of working on. 'It is whilst you are cleaning a car that you can spot things which can be improved upon,' he said to his mechanics. Then, as they hadn't got time to go back to the hotel to eat, Joseph brought them their meal in their little workshop. 'He never gives himself airs — I don't think he always remembers that he is a great driver,' Ugo told me.

The race on Sunday was a success again. Seppi took a second place, this time behind Revson.

When he got back to Europe, Siffert put his business affairs in order and in particular sorted out the details of an office block which he was building in the middle of Fribourg.

For the Italian Grand Prix at Monza he was one of the chief favourites. After a good start, Seppi realized that his BRM was tending to overheat. So he fell back a bit from the leading pack which was made up of Regazzoni, Stewart, Peterson and Cevert. Then, on lap 20, when the water temperature had gone back to normal, Siffert had a go at the group and got past, pulling away from them. By the 30th lap of the 55 laps, he was over 300 yards in front of the pursuit. Was Siffert going to win the Italian Grand Prix out on his own — a rare achievement in which only Jim Clark had succeeded in recent years? No. One lap later, slowing for the Parabolica, the selector fork in the gearbox stuck in fourth gear. Seppi ran the remaining 24 laps without changing gear, stuck in fourth, and finished the race in ninth position. 'If I had had the gearbox out of your Cadillac, I would certainly have won,' he told his friend, Georges Blanc, after the race.

For the Can-Am at Donnybrook in Minnesota, Ugo and Eddy played a joke on Seppi and made him an apple-pie bed. However, Seppi arrived a day later than expected and his room was taken by an elderly couple who perhaps did not have an exactly enjoyable surprise!

Siffert had one himself, but in the race, when as he was lying third, his Porsche ran out of petrol five hundred yards from the finish, which cost him two places. In spite of this incident, the Swiss driver took a third place in the general classification, doing better than Jackie Stewart.

Simone and Veronique rejoined their husband/father at Mosport for the Canadian Grand Prix in the most appalling weather. Seppi spun off twice in practice, and then spun right off the track on the first lap of the race. Covered in mud and able to see nothing beyond his visor, he stopped for a few moments at the pits to sort himself out and to tidy up the nose of his BRM, and finally finished the race ninth.

During the weekend he signed a new contract with BRM for the 1972 season. For sports cars the choice was restricted as Porsche had announced their retirement, and it looked as if Siffert would do a deal with Alfa-Romeo.

Fourth in the Can-Am race at Edmonton in Canada, Siffert was overtaken by one point by Stewart in the general classification. But there were still two races to go and, as the bulk of the prize money was shared between the first three places, the battle looked like being a hot one.

Seppi was calm and relaxed for the weekend of the United States Grand Prix at Watkins Glen. The BRM had not proved entirely satisfactory during practice, but unlike the year before his worries over contracts for 1972 had disappeared already, and the presence of his daughter Veronique and Simone gave him a lot of pleasure.

The evening before the race, we ate in the restaurant of the motel where all the drivers were staying. At the next table, Jackie Stewart and Rob Walker were having a great discussion with the chaplain of the Watkins Glen circuit. After a good half-hour's conversation, the Reverend went off: Seppi turned to Jackie; 'Have you signed up a new publicity contract with the house he represents?' asked the Swiss, pointing his finger towards heaven.

Stewart roared with laughter. That blessed Seppi always had a joke. The two men got on well and there was a kind of mutual respect between them. 'Some people think he is very serious,' Stewart told me. 'In fact not many people know how funny he can be and what a nice chap he is.'

As Seppi, so did Jackie work hard. If the money was not too difficult to earn, it did not come in by itself. Stewart and

Siffert were the real modern drivers, thorough, knowing how to get the best out of their position. They were professionals.

As soon as we had eaten, a large delegation from the Swiss colony of New York transformed the saloon bar in the basement into a real Swiss chalet: accordion, flags, folk songs gave the bar a festive air which the Americans rather liked. When, in a simple and friendly way, Seppi came and greeted them, they were enchanted . . .

The race next day went well; lapping consistently Seppi carried off a good second place behind Francois Cevert whose first Formula One victory it was.

This race was the last round of the Drivers' World Championship; following the death of Pedro Rodriguez the organizers of the Mexican Grand Prix had decided not to hold the race that year. With 19 points, Jo Siffert was fourth in the final classification for the World Championship — equal with Jacky Ickx.

After his return to Fribourg, he crossed the Atlantic once again a week later to take part in a Can-Am at Laguna Seca in California which he finished in fifth place on the Porsche 917/10 — of which the engine had been stripped down and re-assembled after every single race in the series.

In the evening, Seppi was invited to a big reception. Acting on his orders, Eddy and Ugo went with him. The two mechanics were a little unhappy; only the driver had received an invitation. 'If anyone stops us, I won't go either,' he said, and the three inseparables went in as one man!

Meeting up with Joseph again on the following Tuesday at Zurich, where two signing sessions were on the agenda, I did not conceal my doubts about his third place in the final classification for the Can-Am Series. The last remaining race would be held on the very fast Riverside circuit where he would be on the very fast Riverside circuit where he would be very pushed to beat Stewart's Lola. 'Stewart is too much of a favourite to win,' Seppi replied. 'He's bound to retire.'

One race, held on the Sunday at Brands Hatch in honour of the World Champion, Jackie Stewart. For once, Seppi was not very keen to race. He was feeling a bit fed-up with it — with forty races, the 1971 season had been a full one. The next day, knowing that several offers had already been made to him and in particular that one which he had refused had come back again in spite of it, I had a word with him.

'About your book, I have my ideas but I would like to talk them over with you as soon as possible.'

'All right,' Seppi agreed, 'we will look into it as soon as the season is over. In the meantime I have been working out an exact list of all my journeys this year: I would like you to calculate the distances and the numbers of hours in the air — I think we have done even more than I did in 1969.'

The next day Siffert left for Stuttgart and then London, from where he travelled down to Brands Hatch. His BRM was running beautifully and the Swiss put in fastest time in practice, which put him in pole position on the starting grid. An advantage on other circuits, this position was a bit of a handicap at Brands Hatch: it was a little lower on the track in a sort of dip from which the car had some difficulty in extracting itself.

On the 24th October Siffert made a bad start, then put his right wheel onto the grass to avoid Peterson who was coming through. Lying tenth after some 200 yards of the race, he started to climb up through the field in his own inimitable way; on the fourteenth lap he was fourth. After a hold-up overtaking another car, Siffert lost a second on the fifteenth lap. As in Austria, it is possible that a tyre had started to go down. On the sixteenth lap, the BRM went into the long left-hander behind the pits, holding right over to the left ready for the next right turn, down the straight of Pilgrims Drop. Suddenly John Surtees, who was two seconds behind, saw the car zigzag over the track just before the dip. The damaged tyre had gone down. Suddenly the BRM swung to the left and hit the protecting bank, bounced back onto the track where it then hit the signal-board at Hawthorn Corner. The BRM bounced into the bank again, losing the tank on its left side and turned over; hurled into the air, it went over a marshal's hut and then came down, crashing to the ground, where it exploded. Jammed in the cockpit, his left leg badly broken, apparently unconscious, Joseph Siffert died almost instantly, asphyxiated without pain.

As Surtees, one of his tyres ripped by some of the debris from the BRM scattered when it hit the bank the first time, crawled back to his pit, the other machines were stopped. For the first time over a long period a race had had to be stopped following an accident . . .

The engines were silenced. In the stands and around the circuit an awful quiet succeeded their roar.

Help was not very quick in coming; two of the three fire extinguishers at the site of the drama did not work. But in any case it was too late. On this day Seppi did not have another chance. He had used up his last ticket.

'At a time like this I defy anyone to find any sense in our profession,' declared Jackie Stewart.

* * * * *

Nearly 50,000 people attended the funeral of Jo Siffert on 29th October at Fribourg. Behind the hearse, Jean-Pierre Oberson carried the red helmet with the white cross. Then, silent now, followed the Porsche 917.

The man they buried that day had proved that in motor sport and in life one can attain any end on which one can reasonably set one's sights if one has the will, the determination and the capacity to succeed. Of this Jo Siffert was a striking example. Racing was his life and death, and he was happy.

199

APPENDIX
RACING RESULTS

Date	Epreuve	Place	Car	Co-drive
	1960			
13.2	Ice Slalom (Lac Noir)	34th	Jaguar	
3.7	Reims Coupe Junior	7th	Stanguellini	
31.7	Messina Grand Prix	4th	Stanguellini	
14.8	Sierre-Montana Hill-climb	7th	Stanguellini	
21.8	Urcy Hill-climb	7th	Stanguellini	
28.8	GP de la Montagne (Swiss)	2nd	Stanguellini	
11.9	Gaisberg Hill-climb	6th	Stanguellini	
18.9	Mont-Verdun Hill-climb	5th	Stanguellini	
	1961			
19.3	Mont-sur-Rolle Hill-climb	1st	Lotus 18	
2.4	Cesenatico Trophy	1st	Lotus 18	
9.4	Vallelunga Grand Prix	2nd	Lotus 18	
16.4	Lake of Garda Grand Prix	1st	Lotus 18	
30.4	Eifel Grand Prix (Nurburgring)	1st	Lotus 18	
14.5	*Monaco Grand Prix*	5th	Lotus 18	
21.5	Grand Prix des Frontieres (Chimay)	3rd	Lotus 20	
28.5	Oulton Park	9th	Lotus 20	
28.5	Nurburgring 1000 Km	3rd	Ferrari	R. Jenny
4.6	Rouen-les-Essarts Grand Prix	4th	Lotus 20	
11.6	Terramo Grand Prix	1st	Lotus 20	
18.6	Caserta Grand Prix	2nd	Lotus 20	
25.6	Mont-Ventoux Hill-climb	1st	Lotus 20	
2.7	Reims Meeting	3rd	Lotus 20	
23.7	Messina Grand Prix	Accident	Lotus 20	
27.8	Enna Grand Prix	1st	Lotus 20	
3.9	Cadours Hill-climb	1st	Lotus 20	
8.10	Coupe du Salon (Monthlery)	3rd	Lotus 20	
15.10	Coupe de Paris (Monthlery)	1st	Lotus 20	

1961: European Formula Junior Champion
(Official title — equal with Tony Maggs)
Winner of the Junior World Trophy.

Races counting for the Drivers' World Championship are in italics; MCW signifies races counting for the Sports Car Manufacturers' World Championship. A signifies retirement.

Date	Epreuve	Place	Car	Co-driver
	1962			
18.3	Cesenatico	1st	Lotus 22	
25.3	Lake of Garda Grand Prix	A	Lotus 22	
1.4	Brussels Grand Prix	6th	Lotus 22 1500cc	
15.4	Vienna Grand Prix	1st	Lotus 22	
23.4	Pau Grand Prix	6th	Lotus 22	
13.5	Avus Grand Prix (Berlin)	1st	Lotus 22	
20.5	Naples Grand Prix	Unqualified	Lotus 24-Climax	
2.6	*Monaco Grand Prix*	Unqualified	Lotus 24-Climax	
17.6	*Belgian Grand Prix* (Spa)	10th	Lotus 24-Climax	
1.7	Reims Grand Prix	9th	Lotus 24-Climax	
8.7	*French Grand Prix* (Rouen)	A	Lotus 24-BRM V8	
15.7	GP de la Solitude (Stuttgart)	A	Lotus 24-BRM V8	
5.8	*German Grand Prix*	12th	Lotus 24-Climax	
15.8	Mediterranean Grand Prix (Enna)	4th	Lotus 24-BRM V8	
25.8	GP de la Montagne (Swiss)	1st	Lotus 24-Climax	
2.9	*Italian Grand Prix*	Unqualified	Lotus 24-BRM V8	
2.10	Chamrousse Hill-climb	1st	Lotus 24-Climax	
	1963			
23.3	Snetterton	Accident	Lotus-BRM	
15.4	Pau Grand Prix	A	Lotus-BRM	
21.4	Imola Grand Prix	2nd	Lotus-BRM	
25.4	Syracuse Grand Prix	1st	Lotus-BRM	
12.5	Spa 500 Km	3rd	Ferrari GTO	
26.5	*Monaco Grand Prix*	A	Lotus-BRM	
9.6	*Belgian Grand Prix*	A	Lotus-BRM	
23.6	*Dutch Grand Prix*	7th	Lotus-BRM	
30.6	*French Grand Prix* (Reims)	6th	Lotus-BRM	
20.7	*British Grand Prix*	A	Lotus-BRM	
27.7	GP de la Solitude	A	Lotus-BRM	
4.8	*German Grand Prix*	9th	Lotus-BRM	
18.8	Mediterranean Grand Prix (Enna)	5th	Lotus-BRM	
24.8	GP de la Montagne (Swiss)	2nd	Lotus-BRM	
1.9	Austrian Grand Prix	A	Lotus-BRM	
8.9	*Italian Grand Prix*	A	Lotus-BRM	
21.9	Oulton Park Gold Cup	11th	Lotus-BRM	
29.9	Schauinsland Hill-climb	2nd	Lotus	
5.10	*United States Grand Prix*	A	Lotus-BRM	
27.10	Mexican Grand Prix	9th	Lotus-BRM	

1963: 14th in the Drivers' World Championship with 1 point.

Date	Epreuve	Place	Car	Co-driver

1964

Date	Epreuve	Place	Car	Co-driver
14.4	Syracuse Grand Prix	Accident	Lotus-BRM	
2.5	Silverstone Trophy Race	11th	Lotus-BRM	
10.5	*Monaco Grand Prix*	8th	Lotus-BRM	
24.5	*Dutch Grand Prix*	13th	Brabham-BRM	
31.5	Nurburgring 1000 Km (MWC)	8th	Porsche 2000	H. Schiller
14.6	*Belgian Grand Prix*	A	Brabham-BRM	
28.6	*French Grand Prix* (Rouen)	A	Brabham-BRM	
5.7	Reims 12-Hour	A	Porsche 2000	H. Schiller
5.7	Reims Grand Prix (F2)	7th	Brabham-Cosworth	
11.7	*British Grand Prix*	11th	Brabham-BRM	
19.7	GP de la Solitude	7th	Brabham-BRM	
2.8	*German Grand Prix*	4th	Brabham-BRM	
9.8	Schauinsland Hill-climb	3rd	Ford-Cobra	
16.8	Mediterranean Grand Prix (Enna)	1st	Brabham-BRM	
23.8	*Austrian Grand Prix*	A	Brabham-BRM	
6.9	*Italian Grand Prix*	7th	Brabham-BRM	
00.9	Tour de France	A	Ferrari GTO	D. Piper
4.10	*United States Grand Prix*	3rd	Brabham-BRM	
25.10	*Mexican Grand Prix*	A	Brabham-BRM	

1964: 10th in the Drivers' World Championship with 7 points.

1965

Date	Epreuve	Place	Car	Co-driver
1.1	*South African Grand Prix*	7th	Brabham-BRM	
14.3	Brand Hatch Race of Champions	5th	Brabham-BRM	
4.4	Syracuse Grand Prix	A	Brabham-BRM	
19.4	Goodwood	Accident	Brabham-BRM	
30.5	*Monaco Grand Prix*	6th	Brabham-BRM	
13.6	*Belgian Grand Prix*	8th	Brabham-BRM	
19.6	Le Mans 24 Hours (MWC)	A	Maserati	Neerpasch
27.6	*French Grand Prix* (Clermont-Ferd)	6th	Brabham-BRM	
10.7	*British Grand Prix*	9th	Brabham-BRM	
18.7	*Dutch Grand Prix*	13th	Brabham-BRM	
1.8	*German Grand Prix*	A	Brabham-BRM	
8.8	Enna-Pergusa (F2)	10th		
15.8	Mediterranean Grand Prix (Enna)	1st	Brabham-BRM	
25.8	Les Rangiers Hill-climb	1st	Brabham-BRM	
12.9	*Italian Grand Prix*	A	Brabham-BRM	
3.10	*United States Grand Prix*	11th	Brabham-BRM	

Date	Epreuve	Place	Car	Co-driver
24.10	*Mexican Grand Prix*	4th	Brabham-BRM	
11.12	The Rand Grand Prix (South Afr.)	5th	Brabham-BRM	

1965: 11th in the Drivers' World Championship with 5 points.

1966

1.1	South African Grand Prix	2nd	Brabham-BRM 2000	
25.3	Sebring 12 Hour (MWC)	6th	Porsche-Carrera	C.Voegele
7.4	Pau Grand Prix (F2)	Non-started	Cooper-BRM	
11.4	Goodwood Trophy (F2)	7th	Cooper-BRM	
25.4	Monza 1000 Km (MWC)	5th	Porsche-Carrera	C. Voegele
1.5	Syracuse Grand Prix	A	Cooper-Maserati	
14.5	Silverstone Trophy Race	A	Cooper-Maserati	
22.5	*Monaco Grand Prix*	A	Cooper-Maserati	
5.6	Nurburgring 1000 Km (MWC)	A	Porsche-Carrera	C. Voegele
12.6	*Belgian Grand Prix*	A	Cooper-Maserati	
19.6	Le Mans 24 Hours (MWC)	4th	Porsche-Carrera	C. Davis
	1st Index of Performance			
3.7	*French Grand Prix* (Reims)	A	Cooper-Maserati	
16.7	*British Grand Prix*	A	Cooper-Maserati	
24.7	*Dutch Grand Prix*	A	Cooper-Maserati	
31.7	*German Grand Prix*	Non-started	Cooper-Maserati	
21.8	Les Rangiers Hill-climb	1st	Cooper-Maserati	
4.9	*Italian Grand Prix*	A	Cooper-Maserati	
11.9	Austrian Grand Prix (MCW)	2nd	Porsche-Carrera	
2.10	*United States Grand Prix*	4th	Cooper-Maserati	
23.10	*Mexican Grand Prix*	A	Cooper-Maserati	

1966: 14th in the Drivers' World Championship with 3 points.

1967

2.1	*South African Grand Prix*	A	Cooper-Maserati	
5.2	Daytona 24 Hours (MWC)	4th	Porsche 910	H. Herrmann
12.3	Race of Champions	3rd	Cooper-Maserati	
27.3	Silverstone (F2)	A	BMW T100	
1.4	Sebring 12 Hour (MWC)	4th	Porsche 910	H. Herrmann
23.4	Eifel Trophy (F2)	A	BMW T100	
25.4	Monza 1000 Km (MWC)	5th	Porsche 910	H. Herrmann
29.4	Silverstone Trophy Race	3rd	Cooper-Maserati	

Date	Epreuve	Place	Car	Co-driver
1.5	Spa 1000 Km (MWC)	2nd	Porsche 910	H. Herrmann
7.5	*Monaco Grand Prix*	A	Cooper-Maserati	
14.5	Targa Florio (MWC)	6th	Porsche 910	H. Herrmann
21.5	Syracuse Grand Prix	3rd	Cooper-Maserati	
28.5	Nurburgring 1000 Km (MWC)	A	Porsche 910	H. Herrmann
4.6	*Dutch Grand Prix*	10th	Cooper-Maserati	
11.6	Le Mans 24 Hours (MWC)	5th	Porsche 907	H. Herrmann
	1st Index of Performance			
18.6	*Belgian Grand Prix*	7th	Cooper-Maserati	
25.6	Reims 12 Hour	2nd	Ferrari 330/P3	D. Piper
2.7	*French Grand Prix* (Le Mans)	4th	Cooper-Maserati	
15.7	*British Grand Prix*	A	Cooper-Maserati	
23.7	Mugello, Florence	A	Porsche 910	H. Herrmann
30.7	Brands Hatch 500 Mile (MWC)	3rd	Porsche 910	B. McLaren
6.8	*German Grand Prix*	A	Cooper-Maserati	
20.8	Les Rangiers Hill-climb	1st	BMW T100	
26.8	*Canadian Grand Prix* (Mosport)	Non-started	Cooper-Maserati	
10.9	*Italian Grand Prix*	A	Cooper-Maserati	
24.9	Albi Grand Prix (F2)	A	BMW T100	
1.10	*United States Grand Prix*	4th	Cooper-Maserati	
8.10	Grand Prix of Rome (F2)	9th	BMW T100	
15.10	Paris 1000 Km	5th	Ferrari 330/P3	D. Piper
22.10	*Mexican Grand Prix*	12th	Cooper-Maserati	
29.10	Five World Records (Monza)		Porsche 911 R	R. Steineman
				D. Spoerri
				C. Voegele
12.11	Spanish Grand Prix (Jarama) (F2)	A	BMW T100	

1967: 11th in the Drivers' World Championship with 6 points.

1968

Date	Epreuve	Place	Car	Co-driver
1.1	*South African Grand Prix*	7th	Cooper-Maserati	
3.2	Daytona Beach 24 Hours (MWC)	1st	Porsche 907	Elford-Stomn
		2nd	Porsche 907	H. Herrmann
24.3	Sebring 12 Hour (MWC)	1st	Porsche 907	H. Herrmann
7.4	Brands Harch 500 Mile (MWC)	A	Porsche 907	H. Herrmann
25.4	Monza 1000 Km (MWC)	19th	Porsche 908	H. Herrmann
27.4	Silverstone Trophy Race	A	Lotus-Ford	
28.4	Fribourg Hill-climb	2nd	McLaren-Oldsmobile 4400cc	
5.5	Targa Florio (MWC)	18th	Porsche 907	R. Stommeler

Date	Epreuve	Place	Car	Co-driver
12.5	*Spanish Grand Prix* (Jarama)	A	Lotus-Ford	
19.5	Nurburgring 1000 Km (MWC)	1st	Porsche 908	V. Elford
26.5	*Monaco Grand Prix*	A	Lotus-Ford	
9.6	*Belgian Grand Prix*	7th	Lotus-Ford	
23.6	*Dutch Grand Prix*	A	Lotus-Ford	
30.6	Nuremberg 200 Mile	3rd	Porsche 910	
7.7	*French Grand Prix* (Rouen)	11th	Lotus-Ford	
13.7	Watkins Glen 6 Hour (MWC)	A	Porsche 908	V. Elford
21.7	*British Grand Prix*	1st	Lotus-Ford	
28.7	Mugello, Florence	2nd	Porsche 910	R. Steinemann
4.8	*German Grand Prix*	A	Lotus-Ford	
11.8	Hockenheim	1st	Porsche 910	
15.8	Enna	1st	Porsche 910	
18.8	Les Rangiers Hill-climb	1st	Lotus-Ford	
25.8	Austrian Grand Prix (MWC)	1st	Porsche 908	
8.9	*Italian Grand Prix*	A	Lotus-Ford	
15.9	GP des Nations (Hockenheim)	5th	Porsche 910	
22.9	*Canadian Grand Prix* Mt Tremblant	A	Lotus-Ford	
29.9	Le Mans 24 Hours (MWC)	A	Porsche 908	H. Herrmann
6.10	*United States Grand Prix*	5th	Lotus-Ford	
8.10	Grand Prix of Rome (F2)	9th	BMW	
13.10	Baden-Wurttemberg (F2)	A	BMW	
20.10	Albi Grand Prix (F2)	4th	BMW	
27.10	Grand Prix of Rome (F2)	A	BMW	
3.11	*Mexican Grand Prix*	6th	Lotus-Ford	
1.12	Buenos Aires GP (Temporada)	A	Tecno	
8.12	Cordoba Grand Prix (Temporada)	7th	Tecno	
15.12	San Juan Grand Prix (Temporada)	4th	Tecno	
22.12	Buenos Aires GP (Temporada)	3rd	Tecno	

1968: 7th in the Drivers' World Championship with 12 points.

1969

1.2	Daytona Beach 24 Hours (MWC)	A	Porsche 908	H. Herrmann
1.3	*South African Grand Prix*	4th	Lotus-Ford	
16.3	Brands Hatch Race of Champions	4th	Lotus-Ford	
21.3	Sebring 12 Hours (MWC)	A	Porsche 908	B. Redman
30.3	Silverstone Trophy	11th	Lotus-Ford	
7.4	Thruxton (F2)	A	BMW	
13.4	Brands Hatch 500 Miles (MWC)	1st	Porsche 908	B. Redman

Date	Epreuve	Place	Car	Co-drive
25.4	Monza 1000 Km (MWC)	1st	Porsche 908	B. Redm
27.4	Eifelrennen (F2)	2nd	BMW	
4.5	*Spanish Grand Prix* (Montjuich)	A	Lotus-Ford	
11.5	Spa 1000 Km (MWC)	1st	Porsche 908	B. Redm
18.5	*Monaco Grand Prix*	3rd	Lotus-Ford	
1.6	Nurburgring 1000 Km (MWC)	1st	Porsche 908	B. Redm
8.6	Zolder (F2)	6th	BMW	
14.6	Le Mans 24 Hours (MWC)	A	Porsche 908	B. Redm
21.6	*Dutch Grand Prix*	2nd	Lotus-Ford	
29.6	Reims Grand Prix (F2)	A	BMW	
6.7	*French Grand Prix* (Clermont-Fer.)	9th	Lotus-Ford	
12.7	Watkins Glen 6 Hours (MWC)	1st	Porsche 908	B. Redm
13.7	Watkins Glen (Can-Am)	6th	Porsche 908	
19.7	*British Grand Prix*	8th	Lotus-Ford	
3.8	*German Grand Prix*	5th	Lotus-Ford	
10.8	Austrian Grand Prix (MWC)	1st	Porsche 917	K. Ahrer
17.8	Mid-Ohio, Lexington (Can-Am)	4th	Porsche 917 A	
24.8	Mediterranean Grand Prix (F2)	A	BMW	
31.8	Elkhart Lake, (Can-Am)	A	Porsche 917 A	
7.9	*Italian Grand Prix*	8th	Lotus-Ford	
14.9	Bridgehampton, N.Y. (Can-Am)	3rd	Porsche 917 A	
20.9	*Canadian Grand Prix* (Mosport)	A	Lotus-Ford	
28.9	Irish Hills, Michigan (Can-Am)	4th	Porsche 917 A	
5.10	*United States Grand Prix*	A	Lotus-Ford	
10.10	Japanese Grand Prix	6th	Porsche 917 A	D. Piper
12.10	Laguna Seca (Can-Am)	5th	Porsche 917 A	
19.10	*Mexican Grand Prix*	A	Lotus-Ford	
26.10	Riverside, California (Can-Am)	A	Porsche 917 A	
9.11	College Station, Texas (Can-Am)	4th	Porsche 917 A	

1969: 9th in the Drivers' World Championship with 15 points.
Porsche winner of the Sports Car Manufacturers' World Championship.
4th in the Can-Am Series Final Classification.

1970

31.1	Daytona Beach 24 Hours (MWC)	2nd	Porsche 917	B. Redm
7.3	*South African Grand Prix*	10th	March-Ford	
21.3	Sebring 12 Hours (MWC)	4th	Porsche 917	B. Redm
30.3	Thruxton (F2)	A	BMW 1600	
30.3	Thruxton	1st	Porsche 917	

APPENDIX

Date	Epreuve	Place	Car	Co-driver
12.4	Brands Hatch 1000 Km (MWC)	.A	Porsche 917	B. Redman
19.4	*Spanish Grand Prix* (Jarama)	Unqualified	March-Ford	
25.4	Monza 1000 Km (MWC)	12th	Porsche 917	B. Redman
26.4	Fribourg Hill-climb	1st	Brabham-Repco	
3.5	Targa Florio (MWC)	1st	Porsche 908/3	B. Redman
10.5	*Monaco Grand Prix*	8th	March-Ford	
17.5	Spa 1000 Km (MWC)	1st	Porsche 917	B. Redman
24.5	Zolder (F2)	6th	BMW	
31.5	Nurburgring 1000 Km (MWC)	A	Porsche 917	B. Redman
7.6	*Belgian Grand Prix*	7th	March-Ford	
13.6	Le Mans 24 Hours (MWC)	A	Porsche 917	B. Redman
20.6	*Dutch Grand Prix*	A	March-Ford	
28.6	Grand Prix of Rouen (F2)	1st	BMW	
5.7	*French Grand Prix* (Clermont-Fer.)	A	March-Ford	
12.7	Watkins Glen 6 Hours (MWC)	2nd	Porsche 917	B. Redman
12.7	Watkins Glen (Can-Am)	2nd	Porsche 917	
18.7	*British Grand Prix*	A	March-Ford	
26.7	Paul Ricard Circuit (F2)	A	BMW	
2.8	*German Grand Prix* (Hockenheim)	8th	March-Ford	
16.8	*Austrian Grand Prix*	9th	March-Ford	
23.8	Enna (F2)	2nd	BMW	
30.8	Salzburgring (F2)	A	BMW	
6.9	*Italian Grand Prix*	A	March-Ford	
13.9	Tulln-Langenlebarn (F2)	A	BMW	
20.9	*Canadian Grand Prix*	A	March-Ford	
27.9	Grand Prix of Imola (F2)	A	BMW	
4.10	*United States Grand Prix*	9th	March-Ford	
11.10	Zeltweg 1000 Km (MWC)	1st	Porsche 917	B. Redman
25.10	*Mexican Grand Prix*	A	March-Ford	
1.11	Jarama 6 Hours	3rd	Porsche 908	J. Fernandez
7.11	Kyalami 9 Hours	2nd	Porsche 917	K. Ahrens

1970: Unclassified in the Drivers' World Championship.
Porsche winner of the Sports Car Manufacturers' World Championship.

1971

Date	Epreuve	Place	Car	Co-driver
10.1	Buenos Aires 1000 Km (MWC)	1st	Porsche 917	D. Bell
24.1	Argentine Grand Prix	6th	March-Ford	
31.1	Daytona Beach 24 Hours (MWC)	A	Porsche 917 K	D. Bell
7.2	Colombian Grand Prix (F2)	1st	Chevron	
14.2	Grand Prix of Bogota (F2)	6th	Chevron	

Date	Epreuve	Place	Car	Co-driver
6.3	*South African Grand Prix*	A	BRM P153	
14.3	Mallory Park (F2)	5th	Chevron	
20.3	Sebring 12 Hours (MWC)	5th	Porsche 917	D. Bell
28.3	Questor Grand Prix, Ontario	6th	BRM P160	
4.4	Brands Hatch 1000 Km (MWC)	3rd	Porsche 917	D. Bell
9.4	Oulton Park	A	BRM P153	
12.4	Thruxton (F2)	A	Chevron	
12.4	Thruxton (Sports Car)	1st	Porsche 917	
18.4	*Spanish Grand Prix* (Montjuich)	A	BRM P160	
25.4	Monza 1000 Km (MWC)	2nd	Porsche 917	D. Bell
2.5	Eifellandrennen (F2)	10th	Chevron	
8.5	Silverstone Trophy	A	BRM P160	
9.5	Spa 1000 Km (MWC)	2nd	Porsche 917	D. Bell
16.5	Targa Florio (MWC)	A	Porsche 908/3	B. Redman
23.5	*Monaco Grand Prix*	A	BRM P160	
30.5	Nurburgring 1000 Km (MWC)	2nd	Porsche 917	P. Rodrigue
31.5	Crystal Palace (F2)	A	Chevron	
2.6	Vallelunga	2nd	Porsche 917	
12.6	Le Mans 24 Hours (MWC)	A	Porsche 917 L	D. Bell
20.6	*Dutch Grand Prix*	6th	BRM P160	
27.6	Zeltweg 1000 Km (MWC)	A	Porsche 917 K	D. Bell
4.7	*French Grand Prix* (Le Castellet)	4th	BRM P160	
17.7	*British Grand Prix*	9th	BRM P160	
24.7	Watkins Glen 6 Hours (MWC)	2nd	Porsche 917	G. van Len
25.7	Watkins Glen (Can-Am)	3rd	Porsche 917/10	
1.8	*German Grand Prix*	A	BRM P160	
15.8	*Austrian Grand Prix*	1st	BRM P160	
22.8	Mid-Ohio (Can-Am)	2nd	Porsche 917/10	
29.8	Road-America (Can-Am)	2nd	Porsche 917/10	
5.9	*Italian Grand Prix*	9th	BRM P160	
12.9	Donnybrooke (Can-Am)	5th	Porsche 917/10	
19.9	*Canadian Grand Prix* (Mosport)	9th	BRM P160	
26.9	Edmonton (Can Am)	4th	Porsche 917/10	
3.10	*United States Grand Prix*	2nd	BRM P160	
17.10	Laguna Seca (Can-Am)	5th	Porsche 917/10	
24.10	Brands Hatch *Race Stopped*	4th	BRM P160	

1971: 4th in the Drivers' World Championship with 19 points (Equal with Jacky Ickx).
Porsche winner of the Sports Car Manufacturers' World Championship.
4th in the Can-Am Series Final Classification.